MODERN STOICISM

*Overcome Life's Challenges and Discover
Peace, Joy, and Emotional Strength Through
Ancient Philosophy*

J. T. Wells

First Edition: 2024

Contents

Introduction

I first discovered the philosophy of Stoicism during my time as a Certified Public Accountant (CPA). Working in the accounting and tax field, I was no stranger to stress. Workload demands were high, and time was always short. I was spending more and more time at the office and less with my family. Markets were softening, clients were uneasy and on the verge of panic, and the pressure to produce for my clients was immense. Amid this chaos, I found myself struggling to maintain a clear mind. I needed something to ground me, a framework to help me navigate through the storm. That's when I discovered the ancient philosophy of Stoicism and decided to put these practices to use.

Stoicism offered me a way to control my emotions and focus on what I could control. It taught me to accept the things I couldn't change and to act with courage and wisdom in the face of adversity. These principles didn't just help me survive those challenging times; they helped me thrive. I found peace amid chaos and purpose in the face of uncertainty. This book aims to offer you the same tools and insights that have been invaluable to me.

The Purpose of This Book

The main goal of this book is simple: to guide you in applying Stoic principles to overcome the challenges of modern life. Whether you're dealing with stress at work, conflicts at home, or the existential angst that often accompanies our fast-paced, digitally-driven lives, Stoicism provides a timeless framework for finding peace and purpose. By the end of this book, you will have practical tools and actionable advice to help you navigate life's ups and downs.

About Me

I spent the first part of my career as a CPA in tax and accounting before moving into the banking industry. Over the years, I've encountered countless challenges that tested my resolve and integrity. Stoicism helped me maintain a balanced perspective and make decisions with calm rationality. By embracing Stoic teachings, I've stayed grounded, practiced self-discipline, and focused on what truly matters. It was Stoicism that led me to decide to change careers. The stress of tax was taking a toll on my mental and physical health; by applying Stoic principles, I decided to make a change in my life and move into banking, where I continue to utilize these principles daily. My journey has been one of continuous learning and growth, and I am excited to share these insights with you.

What is Stoicism?

Stoicism is an ancient Greek philosophy founded in the early 3rd century BC by Zeno of Citium. At its core, Stoicism teaches the development of self-control and fortitude as a means to overcome destructive emotions. The philosophy asserts that virtue (wisdom, courage, justice, and temperance) is the highest good. The Stoics believed we should live in harmony with nature and focus on what is within our control while accepting what is not.

Why Stoicism Matters Today

In today's fast-paced world, we are constantly bombarded with information, distractions, and stressors. Anxiety and depression rates are at an all-time high, and many of us struggle to find meaning and purpose in our daily lives. According to a study by the World Health Organization, nearly 264 million people worldwide suffer from depression. Stoicism offers practical tools to help us navigate these challenges. At its heart, it teaches us to remain calm in the face of adversity, and shift our focus inward. These principles are not just theoretical but practical and actionable, making them incredibly relevant for use in modern life.

What to Expect

In the following chapters, we will explore the core principles of Stoicism and how to apply them in various aspects of life. We will begin by discussing how to manage emotions and build self-discipline. Next, we will explore navigating life transitions and finding meaning and purpose. Each chapter will include practical exercises and real-life examples to help you apply these principles in your daily life.

What You Will Gain

By committing to this journey, you will gain a deeper understanding of Stoicism and how it can help you lead a more peaceful and purposeful life. You will learn to manage your emotions, build resilience, and make decisions with greater clarity and wisdom. The practical exercises and actionable advice in this book will empower you to apply Stoic princi-ples in real-life situations, helping you to overcome challenges and achieve a sense of balance and fulfillment.

A Call to Action

I invite you to join me on this journey of self-discovery and growth. Stoicism has the power to transform your life, just as it has transformed mine. By embracing its teachings, you can find peace amid chaos, purpose in the face of life's complexities, and resilience in the face of adversity. Let this book guide you as you navigate the complexities of modern life and strive to become the best version of yourself.

Thank you for taking this first step. Let's begin this journey together.

Chapter 1

Foundations of Stoicism

"Sometimes even to live is an act of courage."

— Seneca

H ave you ever found yourself in a situation where everything feels beyond your control, and the chaos around you seems insurmountable? Without needing to give it much thought, several scenarios from my life, both personal and professional, quickly come to mind. I am sure that will be the same for you. In our modern time, the struggles our ancestors faced should be gone. Their problems should have all been solved with the technology that we now possess, but they were most definitely not. Throughout history, as we have solved one problem, another has risen to take its place. History shows us that our ancestors faced the same emotional and mental crises we face today.

Stoicism has been utilized throughout history for one reason—it works. It is time-tested and proven. Though described as an "ancient philosophy," the core problems our ancestors faced were the same as those we see today. This chapter will introduce you to the rich history and foundational principles of Stoicism, setting the stage for how you can apply these timeless lessons to your own life.

A Brief History of the Origins of Stoicism

Stoicism began during a time of major change in ancient Greece and Rome. After Alexander the Great died in 323 BCE, Greek culture spread widely, and new philosophies emerged, each offering different ideas on how to live a good life. As Greek culture mixed with local traditions, people looked for philosophies that could provide stability and guidance in a world that was becoming more connected and uncertain.

When the Roman Empire rose to power, it further shaped the way people thought. As Rome expanded, there was a lot of cultural exchange and societal upheaval. In response to these changes, philosophies that focused on personal resilience and inner peace became popular. Stoicism, which emphasizes virtue, wisdom, and self-control, resonated with many people facing the challenges of life in a growing and diverse empire.

Stoicism was founded by Zeno of Citium around 300 BCE in Athens. Zeno, originally from Cyprus, ended up in Athens after being shipwrecked. There, he studied under several philosophers before developing his own ideas. He started teaching at the Stoa Poikile, or Painted Porch, which is where Stoicism got its name. Zeno emphasized living in harmony with nature and the importance of rational thinking and virtue.

Cleanthes, who followed Zeno, brought a practical and disciplined approach to Stoicism. A former boxer, Cleanthes was known for his hard work and perseverance. He wrote extensively on Stoic ethics and theology, helping to further develop the philosophy.

Chrysippus, who came after Cleanthes, played a crucial role in organizing and expanding Stoic teachings. He wrote hundreds of works, though only fragments survive today. Chrysippus focused on the logical and ethical aspects of Stoicism, making it one of the most comprehensive and influential schools of thought in the ancient world. His work solidified the intellectual foundation of Stoicism and ensured its survival over the centuries.

Stoicism evolved through three main phases: the Early Stoa, the Middle Stoa, and the Late Stoa. The Early Stoa, represented by Zeno, Cleanthes, and Chrysippus, established the core principles of the philosophy. During the Middle Stoa, Stoic ideas were integrated with other philosophical traditions, like Platonism and Aristotelianism. Notable figures from this period include Panaetius and Posidonius, who adapted Stoicism to fit the Roman way of life.

The Late Stoa, featuring Roman Stoics like Seneca, Epictetus, and Marcus Aurelius, focused on practical ethics and personal resilience. These philosophers played a big role in shaping Stoicism's lasting legacy. Seneca, who was an advisor to Emperor Nero, wrote extensively on ethics and how to live well. His works, such as "Letters from a Stoic," offer practical advice on dealing with challenges and finding inner peace.

Epictetus, a former slave who became a philosopher, taught that true freedom comes from within. His "Discourses" and "Enchiridion" provide valuable insights into focusing on what we can control. Marcus Aurelius, a Roman Emperor and philosopher, wrote "Meditations" as a personal reflection on Stoic principles, showing how Stoicism can be applied in everyday life and leadership.

Key texts like Marcus Aurelius' "Meditations," Seneca's "Letters from a Stoic," and Epictetus' "Discourses" form the foundation of Stoic philosophy. These works have been studied and respected for centuries, offering practical wisdom on how to live a virtuous and fulfilling life. As you explore the history and evolution of Stoicism, you'll see how these ancient teachings are still relevant today, offering practical tools to deal with the challenges of modern life.

The Core Tenets of Virtue, Wisdom, and Logos

Virtue stands at the heart of Stoic ethics, embodying the highest good one can achieve. In Stoicism, virtue is not just moral excellence but the very foundation upon which a fulfilling life is built. The Stoics believe that living virtuously aligns us with our true nature and the rational order of the universe. The four cardinal virtues—Wisdom, Courage, Justice, and Temperance are the pillars of this ethical framework. These virtues guide our actions, shape our character, and help us navigate life's challenges.

Wisdom, represented by the symbolic owl, is perhaps the most crucial of the four virtues, as it informs our decision-making and leads us toward a virtuous life. Wisdom involves the practical application of knowledge to everyday situations, allowing us to act with reason and discernment. It is not merely intellectual understanding but a deeply ingrained ability to make sound judgments. For instance, in my role as a banker, wisdom enables me to assess complex financial situations, visualize and weigh the potential outcomes of a loan action, and decide on the best scenario for my customers. This clarity of thought and purpose is what sets a wise person apart.

Courage, symbolized by the lion, empowers us to face adversity with resilience and strength. It is the inner resolve that allows us to confront fears, take risks, and stand up for what is right, even in the face of over-whelming odds. Courage is not the absence of fear but the ability to act despite it. In my personal and professional life, there have been numerous instances where courage was required, whether making the tough decision to switch careers or telling a client that I cannot offer additional financing. Courage fortifies us, enabling us to persevere and uphold our principles.

Justice, represented by the balanced scales, emphasizes fairness and the equitable treatment of others. It calls for us to act with integrity, respect the rights of others, and contribute positively to our communities. Justice is about more than legal fairness; it is a moral duty to ensure that our actions benefit society as a whole. In the banking industry, justice manifests in transparent dealings, honest communication, and a commitment to serving the best interests of my clients and the bank. Upholding justice not only fosters trust but also cultivates a sense of collective well-being.

Temperance, symbolized by the lotus flower, involves self-control and moderation. It is the ability to regulate our desires, impulses, and emotions to maintain balance and harmony in our lives. Temperance teaches us to appreciate what we have, avoid excess, and focus on what truly matters. Practicing temperance in my daily life helps me maintain a balanced perspective, whether it's managing work-life boundaries or making mindful choices about my health and well-being. This virtue ensures that we remain grounded and centered, even amidst life's temptations and distractions.

The concept of Logos is central to Stoic thought, representing the rational, ordered principle that governs the universe. Logos is often translated as "reason" or "divine reason," underscoring the interconnectedness of all things. The Stoics believed that the universe operates according to a rational and purposeful order, and by aligning ourselves with this natural law, we achieve inner peace and harmony. Understanding Logos helps us accept the unfolding of events, recognizing that everything happens for a reason, even if it is beyond our immediate comprehension.

The interconnectedness of Virtue, Wisdom, and Logos forms a cohesive philosophical system that guides our behavior and decision-making. When we act virtuously, we align with the rational order of the universe, embodying wisdom in our choices. For example, in moments of personal or professional crisis, I rely on these principles to navigate difficult situations with clarity and integrity. By focusing on what is within my control and accepting what is not, I find a sense of peace and purpose that transcends the immediate challenges.

In practical terms, living in accordance with these tenets means consistently applying them to our everyday lives. Whether it's making ethical decisions at work, practicing self-discipline in our personal habits, or maintaining a balanced perspective during a time of uncertainty, these principles offer a roadmap for a fulfilling life. The impact on personal behavior and decision-making is profound, creating resilience, clarity, and a deeper sense of connection to the world around us.

The Stoic Sage

The Stoic Sage represents an ideal of perfect wisdom and virtue, a figure who embodies the highest aspirations of Stoic philosophy. Imagine someone who navigates life's complexities with unwavering rationality, emotional resilience, and ethical integrity. This individual remains calm in the face of adversity, makes decisions guided by reason and virtue, and maintains an inner tranquility that is unaffected by external circumstances. Fleeting emotions or external opinions do not sway the Stoic Sage, but rather they remain steadfast in their commitment to living according to nature and reason.

Key characteristics of the Stoic Sage include perfect rationality and emotional resilience. This means the Sage responds to life's challenges with a clear and logical mind, unclouded by irrational fears or desires. They are emotionally resilient and able to face loss, pain, and disappointment without being overwhelmed. Their sense of self-worth is derived from their internal virtues rather than external achievements or material possessions. In every situation, the Sage acts with wisdom, courage, justice, and temperance, ensuring their actions align with their core values.

However, it's essential to understand that the Stoic Sage is an ideal rather than a realistic goal. No human can achieve perfect wisdom or complete emotional resilience. Instead, the Sage serves as a guiding star, a benchmark against which we can measure our progress and aspirations. The pursuit of becoming a Sage is not about achieving perfection but about striving for continuous improvement. This process involves recognizing our flaws and working diligently to cultivate virtues that bring us closer to the ideal of the Sage.

Ordinary individuals can take practical steps and engage in continuous self-improvement to emulate the qualities of a Stoic Sage. Start by practicing mindfulness and self-reflection to gain a deeper understanding of your thoughts, emotions, and actions. Develop a habit of examining your daily experiences and identifying areas where you can apply Stoic principles. For example, when faced with a stressful situation at work, pause and reflect on how a Sage would respond. Would they act out of anger or frustration, or would they approach the problem with calm rationality and a focus on finding a constructive solution?

Engaging in regular self-improvement activities, such as reading Stoic texts, journaling, and meditating, can help cultivate Sage-like qualities. Seek out opportunities for learning and growth, and be open to feedback and self-assessment. Understand that progress is gradual and that setbacks are part of the journey. By consistently applying Stoic principles in your daily life, you can develop greater emotional resilience, rationality, and alignment with virtue.

Historical and modern examples of individuals who embody Stoic principles can provide inspiration and guidance. Marcus Aurelius exemplified the qualities of a Stoic Sage. As a Roman Emperor, he faced immense challenges, from military conflicts to personal tragedies. Yet, through it all, he maintained a commitment to Stoic principles, as reflected in his personal writings, "Meditations." His reflections on duty, resilience, and the transient nature of life offer timeless wisdom on how to live virtuously in the face of adversity.

In contemporary times, figures such as Viktor Frankl, a Holocaust survivor and psychiatrist, demonstrated Stoic resilience and rationality. In his book "Man's Search for Meaning," Frankl recounts how he found purpose and inner strength amidst the horrors of concentration camps by focusing on what he could control—his attitude and response to suffering. His ability to find meaning and maintain dignity in the most harrowing circumstances is a testament to the power of Stoic principles.

By studying these examples and integrating Stoic practices into our lives, we can strive to embody the qualities of the Stoic Sage. While we will never achieve perfect wisdom or virtue, the pursuit itself is what enriches our lives, bringing us closer to a state of inner peace and fulfillment. The journey toward becoming a Sage is one of continuous learning, self-improvement, and alignment with the values that define who we are and who we aspire to be.

The Dichotomy of Control

In the realm of Stoic thought, few concepts are as foundational and transformative as the Dichotomy of Control. This principle lies at the heart of Stoicism, offering a clear distinction between what we can and cannot control. Understanding this dichotomy can profoundly reshape how we navigate life's challenges. At its core, the Dichotomy of Control teaches us to focus our energy on the aspects of life within our influence —our thoughts, actions, and reactions—while accepting that external events, the actions of others, and natural occurrences lie beyond our control. We can cultivate a sense of peace and purpose by internalizing this concept, even amidst uncertainty and chaos.

Consider further the elements within our control: thoughts, actions, and reactions. These are the domains where we wield actual influence. For instance, our thoughts shape our perceptions and attitudes toward events. We can choose to interpret a setback as a learning opportunity rather than a failure. Our actions, too, are within our control. We decide how we respond to situations, whether with patience or frustration, kindness or hostility. Reactions, the immediate emotional responses we have, can be tempered and guided by mindful reflection. Focusing on these internal factors helps us live with intention and resilience, fostering a sense of empowerment and self-control.

On the other hand, many aspects of life fall outside our sphere of control. External events, such as economic downturns, job loss, political issues, natural disasters, or unexpected illnesses, occur regardless of our wishes. The actions of others, too, are beyond our influence. We cannot dictate how colleagues, friends, or strangers behave. Natural occurrences, like the weather or aging, unfold according to their own rhythms. Accepting these limitations is not about resigning to fate but recognizing the boundaries of our influence. This acceptance can liberate us from unnecessary stress and frustration, allowing us to focus on what truly matters—our internal responses and actions.

In practical terms, applying the Dichotomy of Control can lead to a more peaceful and purposeful life. One technique is to practice mindfulness, a powerful tool for staying present and focused on the things we have control over. For example, during my busiest days at the office, I take a few moments to center myself with deep breathing. This simple act helps me regain clarity, reminding me to focus on my tasks and interactions rather than the overwhelming workload or external pressures. Another technique is cognitive reframing, where we consciously shift our perspective on a situation. Instead of seeing a challenging project as a burden, we can view it as an opportunity to grow and demonstrate our skills.

Real-life scenarios vividly illustrate the effectiveness of the Dichotomy of Control. Imagine a professional facing a sudden job loss. While the loss itself is beyond their control, their response is not. By focusing on what they can control—updating their resume, networking, and exploring new opportunities—they can navigate the situation with resilience and proactive energy. Similarly, in personal relationships, we cannot control how others behave, but we can choose to communicate with empathy and set healthy boundaries. This shift in focus can transform how we handle conflicts, allowing for more constructive and respectful interactions.

The Dichotomy of Control also extends to our daily routines and habits. For instance, we can focus on healthy coping mechanisms like exercise, meditation, and time management to manage stress. These actions are within our control and can significantly improve our well-being. By consistently applying this principle, we can build a more intentional and balanced life, where our energy is directed toward meaningful pursuits rather than wasted on futile attempts to control the uncontrollable.

In essence, the Dichotomy of Control invites us to cultivate a mindset of acceptance and intentionality. It encourages us to embrace our internal power while letting go of external anxieties. This shift in perspective can lead to profound changes in how we experience and respond to life's challenges. By focusing on our thoughts, actions, and reactions, we can navigate any situation with greater peace and purpose, grounded in the wisdom of Stoic philosophy.

The Modern Relevance of Stoicism

The resurgence of Stoicism in contemporary times is not a coincidence. Amid modern life's fast-paced nature, people seek ways to find stability and peace. The rise of self-help and personal development movements has brought Stoic principles back into the spotlight. These movements emphasize the importance of mental well-being, resilience, and personal growth—concepts deeply rooted in Stoic philosophy. Self-help books, podcasts, and seminars often draw from Stoic teachings, presenting ancient wisdom in a modern context. This renewed interest highlights the timeless relevance of Stoicism in addressing the challenges we all face today.

One significant factor contributing to this resurgence is Stoicism's role in modern therapy, particularly Cognitive Behavioral Therapy (CBT). CBT, a widely practiced form of psychotherapy, focuses on changing negative thought patterns to improve emotional well-being. This approach has its roots in Stoic philosophy, which emphasizes the power of rational thinking and the importance of perspective. Techniques used in CBT, such as cognitive reframing and thought challenging, are reminiscent of Stoic practices. By integrating Stoic principles, CBT helps individuals manage anxiety, depression, and other mental health issues, demonstrating the practical applicability of Stoicism in contemporary therapeutic settings.

Stoic principles offer valuable tools for managing stress in our fast-paced world. The demands of a high-paced work environment, navigating family life, managing personal relationships, and the overall demands that society places on us to appear successful are examples everyone can relate to. These forces pulling us in many different directions can leave us feeling overwhelmed and exhausted. Stoicism teaches us to focus on what we can control—our actions, thoughts, and reactions. By applying this principle, we can prioritize tasks, set realistic goals, and approach each day with a sense of calm and purpose. This mindset shift helps reduce stress and guides us toward a more balanced and fulfilling life.

Coping with social media and information overload is another area where Stoicism proves invaluable. In today's digital age, we are bombarded with information, opinions, distractions, and a false sense of reality. This constant influx can lead to anxiety and a sense of being overwhelmed and insufficient. Stoicism encourages us to be mindful of our influences and to focus on what truly matters. We can regain control over our mental space by setting boundaries on social media usage, curating our information sources, and practicing digital detoxes. This intentional approach to digital exposure helps us maintain clarity and focus, reducing the negative impact of information overload.

The benefits of Stoicism for personal growth are profound. Stoic practices can lead to emotional resilience and inner peace, enabling us to navigate life's challenges with grace. My thoughts turn to a boss I once had. He was facing a difficult time in his personal life, just going through a divorce. His work was suffering because of it. At that moment, an aspiring manager decided to go after his position, knowing he was slipping. Unfortunately, it worked out for her. She gained the position, and he lost it. This could have broken him, but he unconsciously put Stoicism into practice. He picked himself up and decided to make some changes in his life. He changed things he could control. He focused on what strengths he had, not his weaknesses. Thankfully, he earned a better position at another company and is doing quite well. Through reflection, mindfulness, and a rekindled sense of gratitude, my ex-boss found purpose again. Stoic teachings helped him reframe his situation, focus on his strengths, and pursue new opportunities with a positive mindset.

To integrate Stoicism into daily routines, consider practical exercises such as journaling, mindfulness meditation, and reflective reading. Journaling allows us to process our thoughts and emotions, providing clarity and insight. Mindfulness meditation helps us stay present and centered, reducing stress and enhancing emotional well-being. Reflective reading of Stoic texts offers timeless wisdom and practical guidance. By incorporating these practices into our daily lives, we can cultivate a Stoic mindset and experience its transformative benefits.

Stoicism's global reach and adaptation across cultures and contexts further highlight its relevance. In business and leadership, Stoic principles are increasingly recognized for their value in fostering ethical decision-making, resilience, and effective leadership. Leaders who embody Stoic virtues inspire trust and respect, creating positive and productive work environments. The influence of Stoic thought extends to modern philosophical discourse, where it continues to shape discussions on ethics, personal growth, and the nature of happiness.

Stoicism provides a powerful framework in which to view the uncertainties and challenges we face. Its principles offer practical tools for managing stress, finding balance, and cultivating resilience. By embracing Stoic teachings, we can achieve a sense of inner peace and purpose, regardless of the challenges we face. As we continue to explore Stoicism's rich legacy, we discover timeless wisdom that empowers us to lead more intentional, fulfilling lives.

Chapter 2

Managing Emotions with Stoicism

"The best answer to anger is silence."

— Marcus Aurelius

I n my early days as a banker, I vividly recall an incident that tested my emotional resilience. I had just taken on a new account that a retiring co-worker passed over to me. During my first review of their financials, it was clear that the client was in trouble. In my very first meeting with this customer, I had to tell them they no longer met the bank's underwriting standards and we could not extend any additional financing to them. I can't imagine a worse first impression, but the conversation with them needed to happen. Naturally, they were very upset with me, and the situation became hostile quickly. My initial reaction was anger and defensiveness. But then, something shifted. I remembered the Stoic teachings I had been studying. Instead of lashing out, I took a deep breath and paused. This small act of restraint allowed me to respond with composure and clarity. The situation calmed down, we worked through a plan, and I still maintain a good relationship with this customer to this day. This chapter will explore how you can harness Stoic principles to manage emotions effectively, starting with one of the most volatile—anger.

Maintain Composure and Control Anger

Anger often arises from specific triggers, such as criticism, perceived injustice, or unmet expectations. Recognizing these triggers is the first step in managing your anger. For example, criticism can feel like a personal attack, sparking a defensive response. Injustice, whether in the workplace or personal life, can ignite a sense of moral outrage. Unmet expectations, such as a project not going as planned, can lead to frustration and disappointment. By identifying these triggers, you can better prepare to handle them when they arise. A helpful exercise is to keep a journal where you note instances of anger, the situations that provoked it, and your reactions. Over time, this practice can reveal patterns and help you develop strategies to manage your anger more effectively.

Once you've identified your anger triggers, the next step is to practice cognitive reframing. This involves changing your perspective on anger-inducing situations. Instead of viewing a challenging scenario as a threat, see it as an opportunity for growth. For instance, if a manager criticizes your work, rather than perceiving it as an attack, consider it a chance to improve and learn. Try to see the situation from the other person's perspective. What might be their underlying concerns or motivations? Using humor can also be a powerful tool to defuse anger. A light-hearted approach can shift the emotional tone of the situation, making it easier to handle.

Developing a pause response is another effective technique for managing anger. Before reacting impulsively, take a moment to pause and breathe, just as I did in the example above. Deep breathing can help calm your nervous system, reducing the intensity of your anger. One simple technique is inhaling deeply through your nose for four seconds, holding your breath for seven seconds, and then exhaling slowly through your mouth for eight seconds. This practice, known as the 4-7-8 technique, can quickly restore a sense of calm. Also, try counting to ten before responding. This allows you to gather your thoughts and choose a more measured response. By pausing, you give yourself the space to respond thoughtfully rather than react emotionally. Immediacy is the ally of uncontrolled emotions; time is its enemy.

Stoic exercises specifically designed to manage anger can also be highly effective. One such practice is negative visualization. This involves imagining the worst-case scenario to reduce the emotional impact of a situation. For example, if you're angry about a project delay, visualize the possible outcomes and how you would cope with them. This exercise can help you realize that even the worst-case scenario is manageable, reducing the intensity of your anger.

Reflecting on the impermanence of the situation is another Stoic technique. Remind yourself that most events are temporary and will pass. I like to visualize our planet, how big it is, and how small I am. A delayed project or failed task will not stop the world from turning. Even the most epic failures in history have been unable to stop it. The world turns, time moves on, and our mistakes become irrelevant. This perspective can help you maintain composure and keep your anger in check.

Reflection Section: Track Anger Triggers Through Journaling

As mentioned above, one practical exercise to help you manage anger is to keep a journal specifically for tracking anger triggers. Each time you feel angry, note the following:

- The situation that provoked your anger
- The specific thoughts and feelings you experienced
- Your initial reaction and any actions you took
- The outcome of the situation

By consistently documenting these details, you can identify patterns in your anger triggers and develop strategies to manage them more effectively. Review this periodically, and you will start to understand your triggers. Use this information to decide how to react when they happen again. Over time, this practice can lead to greater self-awareness and emotional control.

Incorporating these techniques into your daily life can transform how you handle anger. You can maintain your composure even in the most challenging situations by recognizing your triggers, reframing your perspective, pausing before reacting and practicing the Stoic exercise described above. With sustained practice, this approach can greatly help you manage your anger.

Transform Envy into Admiration

Jealousy is an emotion we all encounter at some point, often arising from deep-seated insecurities and constant comparison with others. You might scroll through social media and see someone else's success, sparking a feeling of inadequacy. Or perhaps a colleague receives a promotion you were hoping for, and envy starts to creep in. Understanding the root causes of jealousy is crucial. Insecurity often lies at the heart of jealousy, causing us to doubt our own worth and abilities. Similarly, the fear of missing out (FOMO) can amplify feelings of envy, making us feel as though we're falling behind in the race of life.

Shifting your focus to self-improvement can help mitigate these feelings. Rather than fixating on what others have, concentrate on your growth and progress. Set personal goals that align with your values and aspirations. These goals should be specific, achievable, and meaningful to you. For instance, if you envy a friend's fitness achievements, set a realistic fitness goal for yourself and work towards it. Celebrate your small victories along the way. Each step forward is progress, no matter how minor it may seem. Recognizing and celebrating these achievements can boost your confidence and reduce the power jealousy holds over you.

Cultivating admiration instead of envy is another powerful strategy. When you find yourself feeling jealous of someone, try to identify the qualities or achievements you admire in them. Transform your envy into inspiration. Ask yourself what you can learn from their success. For example, if a colleague receives a promotion and you do not, view it as an opportunity to improve your abilities. Seek feedback, focus on improving your performance, and compare your current work to previous work to view your improvements. Focusing on learning and growth can turn jealousy into a positive, motivating force.

Practicing gratitude can also counteract feelings of jealousy. Gratitude shifts your focus from what you lack to what you have. Start a daily gratitude journaling practice. Each day, write down three things you're grateful for. These could be as simple as a supportive friend, a sunny day, or a personal accomplishment. If you are at a point in life where you feel you have nothing to be thankful for, I will give you three examples right now. You have breath in your lungs, you have a desire to improve your situation, and you have a new day tomorrow. Reflecting on your blessings helps you appreciate your journey and recognize that everyone has their unique path. Over time, this practice can shift your mindset to one of abundance rather than scarcity, reducing the tendency to compare yourself to others.

Reflecting on personal achievements can further diminish jealousy. Take time to acknowledge your milestones and the progress you've made. Create a list of your accomplishments, big and small, and revisit it whenever you feel envious. This exercise reminds you of your strengths and the unique value you bring to the table. By focusing on the things you have accomplished and the growth you've experienced, you will start to cultivate a sense of fulfillment and contentment that jealousy has no hold over.

Reflection Section: Jealousy to Admiration

Take a moment to reflect on someone you feel jealous of. Write down the qualities or achievements you admire in them. Next, identify what you can learn from their success and how you can apply it to your growth. Finally, compile and compare your own gratitude list to this one. Replace your thoughts of jealousy toward others with thoughts of gratitude about your own life. This exercise can help shift your perspective from envy to admiration and gratitude.

Using these strategies, you can transform jealousy from a destructive emotion into a source of motivation and growth. By understanding the root causes, focusing on self-improvement, cultivating admiration, and practicing gratitude, you can navigate jealousy with resilience and poise. This approach can help you manage jealousy and also remind you of the successes in your own life.

Reduce Anxiety with Practical Exercises

Anxiety can be an ever-present shadow lurking in the background of our busy lives. It manifests in various forms—unsettling thoughts, restless nights, or an overwhelming sense of dread. To manage this, the first step is to identify what triggers your anxiety. Uncertainty about the future, social situations, or work pressure are common culprits. These triggers can vary significantly from person to person. Perhaps it's the unpredictability of a project at work or the fear of judgment in social gatherings.

Keeping an anxiety journal can be incredibly helpful. Note down the moments when you feel anxious, the situation you were in, and any specific thoughts or feelings you experienced. Like the anger journal described above, this journal can reveal patterns, helping you understand what consistently provokes your anxiety. I hope you are beginning to see a pattern forming. Journalling will help you know and understand yourself, and the best way to do this is to keep track of what events and situations are difficult for you. This awareness is crucial for developing strategies to manage your emotions.

Engaging in mindfulness practices is another effective way to maintain a calm mind amidst the chaos of daily life. Mindful breathing techniques can anchor you in the present moment, reducing the grip of anxiety. As with anger, we can help calm our minds with one simple method: focus on your breath, inhaling deeply through your nose and exhaling slowly through your mouth. As you breathe, pay attention to the sensations— the rise and fall of your chest, the cool air entering your nostrils, and the warmth as you exhale. This practice can be done anywhere, whether at your desk, in a meeting, or lying in bed. This practice forces us to disengage from the moment and allows time for rational thought to catch up to our emotions.

Another powerful mindfulness practice is the body scan meditation. Lie down or sit comfortably, and systematically bring your attention to different parts of your body, from your toes to your head. Notice any tension or discomfort, and consciously relax each area. This can help you become more aware of your physical state and promote a sense of relaxation and well-being.

Using rational analysis to break down your fears can also alleviate anxiety. Often, our minds jump to the worst-case scenarios, magnifying our fears and making them seem insurmountable. By breaking down these fears into manageable parts, you can better understand and address them. Start by writing down your specific fears and then question their likelihood. For example, if you're anxious about an upcoming flight, an upcoming family event, or a school presentation, ask yourself what the worst possible outcome could be. Is it likely that you miss your flight? Fight with your difficult aunt? Completely bomb the school presentation? Or is it more probable that you make it to your destination without issue, avoid a verbal altercation with your difficult family member (hint: this may be an excellent opportunity to try some of the new techniques you have learned.), or stumble over a few words but still deliver a decent presentation? By dissecting your fears, you can see that they are often less daunting than they initially appear.

Implementing Stoic visualization techniques can further reduce anxiety. Visualizing positive outcomes is a powerful tool. Instead of fixating on what could go wrong, imagine everything going right. Picture yourself catching that flight, successfully de-escalating a difficult family situation, or confidently delivering that presentation, engaging the audience, and receiving positive feedback. This positive visualization can boost your confidence and reduce anxiety.

Another Stoic practice is Premeditatio Malorum, or the premeditation of evils. This involves mentally preparing for potential challenges by imagining the worst-case scenarios. By doing so, you can emotionally brace yourself and develop strategies to cope with these situations if they arise. For instance, if you're anxious about a job interview, imagine the worst possible outcome—a technical glitch, a challenging question, or an unexpected delay. By preparing for these possibilities, you can reduce their emotional impact and feel more in control if they do end up happening. Emotions cannot control the situation if we have already planned for it.

Reflection Section: Anxiety Journal Prompt

To help you identify and manage your anxiety triggers, consider maintaining an anxiety journal. Each time you feel anxious, note the following:

- The situation that triggered your anxiety
- The specific thoughts and feelings you experienced
- Any physical sensations you noticed
- How you responded to the situation

As you can see, this is a similar practice to the one we will be doing to help understand what triggers our anger. Over time, review your entries to identify common patterns and triggers. This practice can increase your self-awareness and help you develop more effective strategies for

managing anxiety.

By recognizing your triggers, engaging in mindfulness practices, using rational analysis, and implementing Stoic visualization techniques, you can develop a robust toolkit for managing anxiety. These strategies can help you traverse the uncertainties of life with a calm and composed mind, which is necessary in the quest for virtue.

Stoic Methods for Daily Peace

Understanding the nature of stress is important in managing it effectively. Stress triggers the body's fight-or-flight response, a physiological reaction that prepares you to either confront or flee from a threat. This response floods your body with adrenaline, which quickens your heartbeat, and sharpens your senses. While beneficial in short bursts, chronic stress can wreak havoc on your health. It can lead to high blood pressure, weakened immune function, and mental health issues like anxiety and depression. Recognizing these effects can motivate you to adopt strategies to mitigate stress and enhance your well-being.

One of the most effective ways to manage stress is to prioritize and simplify tasks. Time management techniques can be invaluable here. Start by creating a to-do list that breaks down your tasks into manageable chunks. Prioritize these tasks based on urgency and importance. Use tools like calendars and apps to schedule your day efficiently. Another critical aspect is learning to say no. I cannot stress this point enough. If you're like me, you have a desire to please everyone, and telling someone no almost feels like you are insulting them. This is far from the truth. Overcommitting can lead to burnout and increased stress. Understand your limits and communicate them clearly to others. By focusing on what truly matters and eliminating unnecessary tasks, you can greatly reduce your stress levels and bring your life back into balance.

Practicing Stoic acceptance can also significantly alleviate stress. This principle involves accepting the present moment as it is, without resistance. Life is full of uncertainties and challenges, many of which are beyond your control. Embracing this reality allows you to focus on what you can control—your actions and reactions. Stoic affirmations can reinforce this mindset. Phrases like "I accept what I cannot change," or "I focus on what I can control," can serve as daily reminders to maintain a balanced perspective. Write one of these phrases on the bathroom mirror or on a sticky note in your car or office. Read this daily as a reminder to yourself. These affirmations can be particularly helpful during stressful situations, reminding you to embrace Stoicism when emotions try to take over.

Incorporating relaxation techniques into your daily routine can further help you unwind and manage stress. Just as we discussed with anxiety, progressive muscle relaxation is a simple yet effective method for stress as well. Tense and then slowly release each muscle group, starting from your toes and working your way up to your head. Relax those muscles along with your mind. Another technique is guided imagery and visualization. Close your eyes and imagine a peaceful scene, such as a serene beach or a quiet forest. Engage all your senses in this visualization—feel the warmth of the sun, hear the gentle waves, and smell the fresh air. I like to imagine my favorite vacation spot and let my mind wander there. This mental escape can provide immediate relief from stress and replace it with a sense of calm.

Emotional Resilience

Life rarely unfolds without a hitch, and setbacks are part of everyone's experience. Developing a growth mindset can transform how you perceive these challenges. Instead of seeing failures as endpoints, view them as opportunities to learn and grow.

History is packed with stories of individuals who turned their failures into stepping stones for success. Take Thomas Edison, who famously said, "I have not failed. I've just found 10,000 ways that won't work." His perspective on failure allowed him to persist, ultimately leading to the invention of the light bulb. Reflecting on your past experiences, consider the lessons you've learned from setbacks. What did you gain from those moments of adversity? How did they shape your path? Always try to find a lesson in every failure; though it may be difficult to see at times, I promise you that it's buried in there somewhere. This reflection can help you see setbacks not as defeats but as valuable learning opportunities. Learning leads us to growth.

Building a support system is equally beneficial on our journey toward emotional resilience. Having a network of friends and family who can offer support, advice, or simply a listening ear can make a significant difference. Sometimes, the mere act of sharing your struggles can alleviate the emotional burden.

Seek out supportive communities or groups where you can connect with others facing similar challenges. These connections can provide a feeling of belonging and shared experience. For example, when I faced professional setbacks or difficult career decisions, confiding in trusted colleagues and friends provided me with new perspectives and encouragement to keep going. Their support reminded me that I wasn't alone in my struggles, and it gave me the strength to persevere. Most of the challenges we face may have already been conquered by someone close to us. Find those people, and you will quickly find they are willing to offer support.

Practicing self-compassion is another essential aspect of emotional resilience. During tough times, it's easy to be overly critical of yourself. However, self-compassion involves treating yourself with the same kindness and understanding you would offer a friend. Engaging in self-compassionate journaling can be a helpful tool. Write about your experiences and emotions without judgment. Acknowledge your efforts and remind yourself that it's okay to struggle. Positive self-talk and affirmations can also reinforce self-compassion. Phrases like "I am doing my best," or "I am worthy of kindness," can help shift your mindset from self-criticism to self-acceptance. This practice of self-forgiveness allows us to move on and grow. Mistakes are inevitable. We can only discover what is and what can be by letting go of what was.

Stoic reflection is another valuable practice for building emotional resilience. Regularly reflecting on your progress and setbacks can provide valuable insight. Take time each evening to review your day. What went well? What could have been improved? This reflection encourages continuous growth and self-awareness. I like to call these "shower thoughts," replaying an event in my head allows me to fully understand my reaction and what brought it about. It also gives me an opportunity to analyze my reaction and decide how I should react in a similar situation going forward.

Writing letters to yourself with encouraging messages can also be a powerful exercise. Imagine writing to a dear friend who is going through a tough time. Offer them support, understanding, and encouragement. Then, read these letters when you need a boost. This practice can also give insight into where you were and how far you have come. Imagine reading a letter written by yourself ten years ago. Would that person from 10 years ago be happy with the person you are today? Now imagine reading a letter in ten years from your current self. What life changes would you hope to see? These practices can help you maintain perspective and focus on growing and learning rather than on failures.

By developing a growth mindset, building a support system, practicing self-compassion, and engaging in regular Stoic reflection, you can cultivate emotional resilience. These strategies equip you to bounce back from setbacks stronger and wiser than you were before. Emotional resilience is not about avoiding difficulties but about facing them with courage. It allows you to navigate life's challenges while discovering inner peace and purpose, grounded in the wisdom of Stoic philosophy.

Chapter 3

Building Self-Discipline and Focus

"No man is free who is not master of himself."

— Epictetus

During the latter years of my career as a CPA, I vividly recall a particularly demanding tax season. The workload was overwhelming, and the staffing wasn't adequate to handle it all. I found myself drifting, struggling to maintain focus, and questioning my ability to stay disciplined. Then, one evening, I sat down with a journal and began to reflect on my core values and long-term goals. This exercise became a turning point. I realized that aligning my actions with my core values was a powerful motivator. I decided that my short-term goal would be to do what needed to be done to finish out the season, with a long-term goal of moving into another area of finance before the next tax season. By setting clear, actionable goals, I was able to regain my focus and discipline, finish out the tax season, and then pursue another career. This chapter will guide you through the process of building self-discipline and focus, starting with the fundamental step of aligning your actions with your core values.

Set Goals that Align with Your Core Values

Identifying your core values is essential for setting meaningful goals in order to help us maintain focus. Core values are the fundamental beliefs and principles that guide your actions and decisions. They serve as your internal compass, helping you navigate life's challenges with integrity and purpose. Consider what made those moments significant. Were there specific principles or beliefs that were honored or violated? For example, if you felt immense satisfaction after helping a friend or colleague, your core value might be compassion or teamwork. Conversely, if you felt distressed by a situation where honesty was compromised, integrity might be a core value for you.

Reflection Section: Identify Core Values

To help you identify your core values, try this simple exercise:

1. Take a blank sheet of paper and divide it into two columns.
2. In the left column, list past experiences that brought you joy, satisfaction, or a sense of achievement.
3. In the right column, note the core values honored in those experiences.
4. Repeat this process for distressing experiences, identifying the values that were violated.

This exercise will help you create a comprehensive list of your core values, providing a solid foundation for goal setting. If you are struggling to identify your core values, fear not; we will discuss these in more detail in Chapter 6.

Once you've identified your core values, the next step is to set SMART goals—goals that are Specific, Measurable, Achievable, Relevant, and Time-bound. This framework ensures that your goals are clear and attainable. For example, if one of your core values is health, a SMART goal might be: "I will run three times a week for 30 minutes each session over the next three months." This goal is specific (running), measurable (three times a week for 30 minutes), achievable (considering your current fitness level), relevant (aligned with your value of health), and time-bound (three months).

Aligning your goals with your core values is crucial for maintaining motivation and focus. When your goals reflect your fundamental beliefs, you are more likely to stay committed and resilient in the face of challenges. To ensure alignment, create a value-goal alignment chart. List your core values in one column and your goals in the adjacent column. For each goal, note how it aligns with your values. This visual representation can help you see the connection between your values and objectives, reinforcing your commitment.

Consider Sarah, a marketing manager who values creativity and innovation. She set a goal to develop a new marketing campaign for her company. By aligning this goal with her core values, she found it easier to stay motivated and focused, even when faced with setbacks. Her value-goal alignment chart showed how each step of the campaign honored her creativity and innovation, providing a constant reminder of why her goal mattered. She aligned her career goals with her core values, allowing her to thrive and find worth in her work.

Breaking down larger goals into actionable steps is another crucial aspect of effective goal setting. Large goals can often feel overwhelming, making it difficult to know where to start. By dividing these goals into smaller, manageable tasks, you can create a clear roadmap to success. Start by creating a step-by-step action plan. List each task required to achieve your goal and arrange them in a logical sequence. For example, if your goal is to write a book, your action plan might include tasks like research, outlining chapters, writing a certain number of words daily, and editing drafts.

Weekly and daily task lists can help you stay organized and focused. Review your action plan each week and create a list of tasks to complete. Break these tasks down further into daily lists, specifying what you will accomplish each day. This approach ensures consistent progress toward your goal, one step at a time. By focusing on small, manageable tasks, you can maintain momentum and avoid feeling over-whelmed.

Reflection Section: Value-Goal Alignment Chart

To create your value-goal alignment chart, follow these steps:

1. List your core values in the first column.
2. In the adjacent column, write down your goals.
3. For each goal, note how it aligns with your core values.

This chart will serve as a visual reminder of the connection between your values and objectives, helping you stay motivated and focused.

By identifying your core values, setting SMART goals, aligning your goals with your values, and breaking them down into actionable steps, you can build self-discipline and focus. These strategies can see you through the challenges in your professional and personal life, and can help you find more purpose and fulfillment by aligning actions with core values.

Structure Your Day for Maximum Productivity

Time-blocking is a method of dividing your day into blocks dedicated to specific tasks. This approach helps you stay focused, organized, and productive. You can create a structured environment that minimizes distractions and enhances concentration by allocating set periods for different activities. Imagine your day as a series of appointments with yourself, each block dedicated to a particular task or activity. This method not only helps you manage your workload but also ensures that you allocate time for essential activities such as breaks, exercise, and personal projects.

The benefits of time-blocking are numerous. For one, it reduces decision fatigue. By pre-scheduling your tasks, you eliminate the need to constantly decide what to do next. This allows you to channel your mental energy into the tasks themselves rather than the process of orga-nizing them. Additionally, time-blocking helps you maintain focus.

Knowing you have a limited time to complete a task creates a sense of urgency that can enhance your productivity. This method also allows you to balance your work and personal life better, ensuring you allocate time for both.

Planning your day in advance is a crucial step in effective time-blocking. Each evening, take a few minutes to outline your schedule for the next day. Start by listing all the tasks you need to accomplish. Then, prioritize these tasks based on their importance and deadlines. Assign specific time blocks to each task, allocating enough time for each activity. Creating a daily time-blocking template can be incredibly helpful. This template serves as a visual guide, allowing you to see your entire day at a glance. Use color coding to differentiate between various types of tasks, such as work-related activities, personal errands, and leisure time.

Incorporating buffer time between tasks is another essential aspect of time-blocking. Buffer time acts as a cushion, allowing for breaks and unexpected interruptions. Without buffer time, even minor delays can throw off your entire schedule. Aim to include short breaks between each time block, such as five to ten minutes to stretch, grab a drink, or simply rest your eyes. Additionally, allocate longer buffer periods for tasks prone to overruns or requiring significant mental effort. For example, if you have a two-hour block dedicated to a complex project, include a 15-minute buffer afterward to decompress and prepare for the next task.

Regular review and adjustment of your time blocks is necessary to ensure ongoing effectiveness. At the end of each week, take some time to assess how well your time-blocking strategy worked. Did you complete your tasks as planned? Were there any time blocks that consistently ran over or under the allocated time? Use this feedback to make necessary adjustments for the following week. If you find that certain tasks require more time than initially estimated, adjust your future time blocks accordingly. Conversely, if some activities take less time, redistribute that extra time to other tasks or use it for additional breaks.

During hectic times at work, typically stemming from multiple time-sensitive loans that all need to be booked around the same time. I implement a rigorous time-blocking strategy. Each evening before heading home, I plan my next day, allocating specific blocks for each customer to ensure I keep all my projects on track and moving forward together. I include buffer times between each block to account for unforeseen delays, such as phone calls or emails that demand my immediate attention, but most importantly, to prevent burnout. At the end of each week, I review my schedule, noting what worked and what needed adjustment. I can honestly tell you that most of my reviews lead to adjustments.

It's impossible to foresee every little interruption. But before implementing time-blocking, I was far less productive. This continual review process allows me to refine my approach weekly, leading to increased productivity and reduced stress. After implementing this process, I became much more effective in my position. Before implementing time-blocking, completing multiple loans on a deadline was almost impossible; now, I can handle more than double the workload without any problems and still come home to my family on time.

Time-blocking is a powerful tool for structuring your day and maximizing productivity. By planning your day in advance, incorporating buffer time, and regularly reviewing your schedule, you can create a balanced and effective time management system. This approach helps you stay focused, reduce stress, and achieve your goals with greater efficiency.

Overcome Procrastination

Procrastination is a challenge many of us face, and understanding its root causes can be the first step in overcoming it. Fear of failure or perfectionism often lies at the heart of our delay tactics. We worry our efforts won't be good enough, so we avoid starting altogether. The thought of not meeting our own or others' expectations can be paralyzing. On the flip side, a lack of clear goals or motivation can also lead to procrastination. When we don't have a specific, compelling reason to take action, it's easy to put things off. The tasks seem vague and impossible, leading us to seek distractions instead. Recognizing these underlying fears and uncertainties can help us address them more effectively.

One powerful tool for combating procrastination is the Two-Minute Rule. This concept is simple yet effective: if a task will take two minutes or less, do it immediately. The idea is to create momentum by immediately tackling small, quick tasks. These could be anything from responding to an email, making a brief phone call, or tidying up your workspace. Promptly handling these minor tasks reduces the clutter in your mind and creates a sense of accomplishment. This momentum can then carry over to larger tasks, making them seem less daunting. For instance, if you're procrastinating on writing a report, start by jotting down a rough outline or a few key points. This small step can break the inertia and make it easier to continue.

Time-blocking, introduced in the previous section, is another effective strategy for overcoming procrastination. By setting aside dedicated time slots for high-priority tasks, you create a structured environment that encourages focus and productivity. The Pomodoro Technique is a popular time-blocking method involving working in short, focused intervals. Typically, you work for 25 minutes (one Pomodoro) and then take a five-minute break. After four Pomodoros, you take a longer break of 15 to 30 minutes. This approach helps maintain concentration while preventing burnout. During each Pomodoro, eliminate distractions and focus solely on the task at hand. The breaks provide a mental reset, making it easier to return to work with renewed energy.

Creating accountability mechanisms can further enhance your ability to combat procrastination. One effective method is to partner with an accountability buddy. This could be a friend, colleague, or family member who shares similar goals. Regular check-ins with your accountability partner can provide mutual support and motivation. For example, you might agree to update each other on your progress every week, discussing any challenges or successes. Knowing that someone else is aware of your commitments can provide the extra push needed to take action. Publicly committing to deadlines is another powerful accountability tool. Whether announcing your intentions on social media or sharing them with your team at work, making your goals known to others increases your sense of responsibility.

In my own experience, I found that combining these strategies creates a powerful framework for overcoming procrastination. For instance, when facing the quarter-end crunch in banking, I like to apply the Two-Minute Rule to any emails requesting my attention, which, as any professional knows, can be quite an overwhelming amount. If I can't complete the task quickly, that email gets bookmarked and sent to the back of my project list. I also use this rule to knock out projects that need only the finishing touches to complete. I then use time-blocking to allocate focused intervals for more time-intensive projects, incorporating short breaks to maintain my energy. Partnering with a close colleague for regular progress check-ins helps keep me accountable and motivated.This multi-faceted approach transformed a daunting number of projects into manageable steps, allowing me to complete them efficiently and effectively.

Understanding the root causes of procrastination, implementing the Two-Minute Rule, using time-blocking techniques, and creating accountability mechanisms are all powerful tools for taking immediate action. By addressing the fears and uncertainties that lead to procrastination and employing practical strategies to overcome them, you can boost your productivity and achieve your goals with greater ease.

Stay Focused by Avoiding Distractions

Recognizing the sources of distraction is a critical first step in maintaining focus. Digital distractions like social media and email are among the most pervasive. They constantly vie for your attention with notifications, alerts, and endless streams of information. Every ping and buzz can pull you away from your work, fragmenting your concentration. It's not uncommon to start a task only to find yourself scrolling through a social media feed minutes later, wondering where the time went. Environmental distractions also play a significant role. Whether it's the noise from a bustling office, the hum of household activities, or even the clutter on your desk, these elements can disrupt your flow and reduce productivity.

Creating a distraction-free environment can significantly enhance your ability to focus. Start by setting up a dedicated workspace. If possible, choose a quiet area where you can work uninterrupted. Keep this space organized and clutter-free; a tidy environment can promote a clear mind. Consider using noise-canceling headphones to block out background noise or playing white noise to create a consistent auditory backdrop. I like to listen to relaxing spa music, which I am actually doing right now as I write this book! These small adjustments can make a big difference in your ability to concentrate. Additionally, establish clear boundaries with those around you. Let family members or colleagues know when you need uninterrupted time, and consider using the "do not disturb" sign or signal to remind them of this.

Digital detox strategies are essential for reducing the impact of digital distractions. Designate specific times or zones as tech-free. For example, make it a rule to avoid checking your phone during meals, the first hour after waking up, or the hour before you go to bed. These tech-free periods can help you reclaim your focus and reduce the constant pull of notifications. Using your device's "do not disturb" feature or using apps to limit screen time can also be beneficial. These tools can provide the structure you need to resist the lure of digital distractions and maintain concentration.

Single-tasking, the practice of focusing on one task at a time, can dramatically improve your productivity. Multitasking, contrary to popular belief, often reduces efficiency and increases errors. Concentrating on a single task allows you to give it your full attention and complete it more effectively. Techniques for maintaining this focus include setting specific goals for each task and using timers to create a sense of urgency. For example, decide to work on a particular report for 30 minutes without interruption, then take a short break before moving on to the next task. This approach can help you maintain a high level of concentration and prevent your mind from wandering.

Scheduling deep work sessions is another great strategy for staying focused. Deep work refers to periods of intense, focused activity where you tackle cognitively demanding tasks. To implement this, block out chunks of time in your calendar specifically for deep work. During these sessions, eliminate all potential distractions, including turning off your phone and closing unnecessary browser tabs. Focus solely on the task at hand, whether it's writing, analysis, or problem-solving. By dedicating regular time to deep work, you can significantly enhance your productivity and the quality of your output.

During particularly challenging periods, I've found these strategies invaluable. For instance, when preparing for a presentation to a big financing prospect, I set up a quiet workspace and use noise-canceling headphones to block out office chatter. I designate tech-free times, checking emails only at scheduled intervals. This prevents constant interruptions and allows me to dive deep into my financing pitch and the presentation I prepare along with it. By focusing on one task at a time and scheduling dedicated deep work sessions, I am able to prepare for the interaction thoroughly and enter the meeting fully prepared. These practices improve my productivity, reduce stress, and calm my nerves because I am now fully prepared for the meeting.

Recognizing and mitigating distractions is crucial for maintaining focus in today's noisy world. By identifying common distractions, creating a distraction-free environment, implementing digital detox strategies, practicing single-tasking, and scheduling deep work sessions, you can enhance your ability to concentrate and achieve your goals more effectively. Reducing distractions provides direction and purpose, allowing for a much more productive day.

Be Consistent

Consistency is the bedrock of achieving long-term goals. Imagine trying to fill a bucket with water by adding a single drop every day. Initially, the progress may seem negligible, but over time, those drops accumulate, eventually filling the bucket. This metaphor illustrates the compound effect of small, consistent actions. Each step, no matter how minor, contributes to the larger goal. The key is maintaining a steady pace and resisting the urge to sprint and burn out. Consistency builds momentum, creates habits, and leads to sustainable success. It's about making incremental progress and trusting that these small efforts will add up.

Building habits gradually is essential for maintaining consistency. Often, we aim for drastic changes, only to find them unsustainable. Instead, start with small, manageable changes. For instance, if your goal is to read more, begin with just five minutes a day. Gradually increase the time as the habit becomes ingrained. Habit-tracking tools can be beneficial in this process. Simple apps like Habitica or even a basic journal can help you monitor your progress. Checking off each day you complete your habit provides a feeling of accomplishment and reinforces the behavior. By focusing on gradual changes, you build a strong foundation for long-term success.

Staying motivated over the long term can be challenging, especially when progress seems slow. Celebrating milestones and progress is crucial for maintaining motivation. Each small win serves as a reminder that you are moving in the right direction. If your goal is to write a book, celebrate completing each chapter. If your goal is to run a mile, celebrate every quarter mile you complete. These celebrations can be simple, like treating yourself to a favorite snack or taking a short break to enjoy an activity you love. Reward yourself for the progress you have achieved. Visualizing long-term benefits can also keep you motivated. Imagine the sense of accomplishment and the positive impact of achieving your goal. This vision can serve as a beacon, guiding you through challenging times. Visualize your goals, then build habits to see them through.

Setbacks and plateaus are inevitable on the path to achieving long-term goals. Developing a plan for overcoming obstacles is necessary for maintaining consistency. When faced with a setback, take a moment to assess the situation. Identify what went wrong and what can be learned from the experience. Then, adjust your approach accordingly. Staying flexible and adapting when necessary is crucial. Rigidity can lead to frustration and burnout, while adaptability allows you to navigate challenges with resilience. Remember that setbacks are a natural part of the process, not a reflection of your capabilities. Forgive yourself for setbacks, and then move on. By maintaining a flexible mindset, you can overcome obstacles and continue moving forward.

In my own career, I've faced numerous setbacks that tested my resolve. One such instance was when I was passed over for a promotion that I really felt I deserved. Initially, I felt disheartened, questioning my ability compared to my peers. However, by taking a step back and reassessing the situation, I developed a new plan. I dove deep into my annual review and made a list of items I needed to improve. I also reached out to my manager and set up an additional meeting to set a clear path on what I needed to do to earn a promotion. I set a goal to make the adjustments I needed to. I changed how I did some things, and these actions eventually became habits. This experience reinforced the importance of flexibility and adaptability in maintaining consistency. Despite the initial setback, I earned my promotion the following year, and the lessons learned proved invaluable.

Consistency is the key to achieving long-term success. By understanding its importance, building habits gradually, staying motivated, and overcoming setbacks, you can maintain a steady path toward your goals. These strategies not only enhance your productivity but also foster resilience and confidence. As you continue to apply these principles, consistency will become a natural part of your routine, leading to sustained success.

In the next chapter, we'll explore how to navigate life transitions with Stoic principles, ensuring that you remain grounded and resilient during times of change.

Chapter 4

Navigating Life Transitions

"Every new beginning comes from some other beginning's end."

— Seneca

T ransitions often come unannounced, shaking the foundation of our comfort zones. I remember a significant turning point in my life when I switched from accounting to banking. While looking for a career change, I interviewed with several companies, but none seemed the right fit. I applied twice to the bank I am with now, both times being rejected for a candidate transferring from another branch. I felt lost and that I had failed in my goal to find a new career in finance. One morning, I got a call from a branch manager of the bank that I had applied to. He said he received my resume from another manager and wanted me to come in for an interview if I was still interested. As you already know, I got the job. But when he offered it to me, it hit me. I am an accountant, not a banker. I hope I didn't just get myself in over my head. The excitement kicked in, but so did the anxiety. It felt like standing on the edge of a cliff, ready to leap into unknown waters. The uncertainty was daunting, but Stoic principles offered a guiding light. This chapter will help you navigate career and life changes with confidence and purpose, turning uncertainty into opportunity.

Find Direction in the Uncertainty of Career Changes

Embracing the present moment is necessary when facing career transitions. Often, we get caught up in what has been or what should have been, neglecting the current opportunities and challenges. Mindfulness exercises can help you stay grounded. Start by taking a few minutes each day to focus on your breath. Inhale deeply, hold for a moment and exhale slowly. Let your thoughts come and go without judgment. This practice can anchor you, providing clarity amid the chaos. Reflect on your current skills and experiences. What have you learned from past roles? How have these experiences shaped your abilities? These reflections can illuminate your strengths, making it easier to see how they apply to new opportunities.

Identifying transferable skills is a good practice considering a career shift. Many skills are versatile and can be adapted to different roles or industries. Start by creating a skills inventory. List all the skills you've acquired in your current and past roles. Include technical skills, such as proficiency in specific software, and soft skills, like communication and leadership. Once you have your inventory, consider how these skills can be applied to new career paths. For example, if you've developed strong project management skills, this ability can be valuable in various industries, from marketing to healthcare. Matching your skills to potential new roles can open up a world of opportunities you might not have considered.

Setting clear and realistic goals is the next step in navigating a career shift. Goals provide direction and motivation, helping you stay focused on what you want to achieve. As discussed previously, use the SMART criteria to set your goals—Specific, Measurable, Achievable, Relevant, and Time-bound. For instance, if you aim to transition into a new industry, a SMART goal might be: "I will complete a certification course in digital marketing within the next six months." This goal is specific (completing a course), measurable (certification), achievable (considering your current knowledge and resources), relevant (aligned with your career transition), and time-bound (six months). Breaking down your goals into actionable steps makes them more manageable. Create a detailed plan outlining the steps you need to take to achieve each goal. This plan can include tasks like researching potential roles, networking, and updating your resume.

Building a support network is invaluable during a career transition. Seek advice and encouragement from mentors, friends, and professional networks. Joining industry-specific groups or forums can provide insights and connections that are helpful on your new path. These groups often host events, webinars, and discussions that can expand your knowledge and network. Additionally, consider seeking guidance from career coaches or mentors. Their experience and perspective can provide valuable advice and support. They can help you navigate the challenges of a career shift, offering strategies and encouragement to keep you moving forward.

Reflection Section: Create a Skills Inventory

To identify your transferable skills, create a skills inventory. List all the skills you've acquired in your current and past roles. Include both technical skills (e.g., proficiency in specific software) and soft skills (e.g., communication, leadership). Once you have your inventory, consider how these skills can be applied to new career paths. Write down potential roles or industries where your skills would be valuable. This exercise can help you see the versatility of your abilities and open up new opportunities.

By embracing the present moment, identifying transferable skills, setting clear and realistic goals, and building a support network, you can navigate career shifts with confidence and purpose. These strategies will help you turn uncertainty into opportunity, guiding you toward a fulfilling and successful career path.

Heal and Move Forward From Broken Relationships

Accepting the end of a relationship is one of the hardest steps in the healing process. It's natural to want to cling to what once was, but holding on can prevent you from moving forward. Stoic exercises for acceptance can be incredibly helpful. Start by practicing the concept of Amor Fati, which means "love of fate." Embrace the breakup as part of your life's journey, even if it's painful. Reflect on the lessons you've learned from the relationship. Perhaps it taught you about your strengths, your boundaries, or what you truly need in a partner. These reflections can turn a painful experience into a valuable learning opportunity.

Practicing self-compassion is crucial during the healing process. It's easy to fall into a cycle of self-blame or harsh criticism, but this only prolongs the pain. Encourage yourself to be kind and gentle with your emotions. Self-compassionate journaling can be a powerful tool. Write about your feelings and experiences without judgment. Allow yourself to express your sadness, anger, or confusion freely. Positive affirmations can also boost your self-esteem. Remind yourself daily that you are worthy of love and happiness. Phrases like "I am enough" or "I deserve peace" can help rebuild your confidence and self-worth.

Focusing on personal growth can transform the breakup into an opportunity for self-improvement. Set personal goals that excite and motivate you. Maybe you've always wanted to learn a new language, take up a hobby, or pursue further education. Engaging in activities that promote self-improvement not only distracts from the pain but also encourages growth and feelings of accomplishment. Hobbies like painting, writing, or hiking can provide a creative and emotional outlet. These activities can help you rediscover your passions and interests, making you feel more connected to yourself.

Cultivating a new social circle is another important step in moving forward. After a breakup, it's common to feel isolated or disconnected. Building new friendships and social connections can fill this void and provide a sense of belonging. Consider joining clubs or groups that align with your interests. Whether it's a book club, a fitness class, or a cooking group, these activities can introduce you to like-minded individuals. Volunteering or community and church involvement can also be incredibly fulfilling. Helping others not only benefits those in need but also gives you a sense of purpose and connection. It's a reminder that you are part of a larger community, and your contributions matter.

Adapt to New Environments When Relocating

Embracing change as an opportunity can transform the daunting task of relocation into a positive experience. Moving to a new place often brings a mix of excitement and anxiety. Reflect on the positive aspects of the move, such as the chance to explore a new area, meet new people, and experience different cultures. Setting goals for your new environment can provide a sense of belonging. Think about what you want to achieve in your new location, whether it's career advancement, personal growth, or simply making your new house feel like home.

Establishing a routine quickly can help you settle into your new environment. Identify key daily activities that bring structure to your day. This might include morning coffee at a local café, a daily walk in a nearby park, or evening visits to the gym. Finding local spots for regular visits can make a new place feel more familiar and comfortable. Over time, these routines will start to make you feel more comfortable in your new environment, making the transition smoother.

Connecting with the community is vital in building a sense of belonging. Attend local events or meetups to meet new people and learn about your new area. Joining community groups, a church or classes can provide opportunities to connect with others who share your interests. These connections can help you feel more integrated into your new environment and offer support during the transition. Building relationships with neighbors and participating in community activities will help you establish new friendships with others that see value you bring to the group.

Staying connected to old friends is equally important. Maintaining relationships with friends and family from your previous location can provide emotional support as you transition to your new home.

Schedule regular phone or video calls to stay in touch. Hand-written letters are also a great way to stay connected with a more personal touch. Planning visits or reunions can give you something to look forward to and help bridge the gap between your old and new environments. Balancing new connections with existing ones can create a supportive network that enables you to navigate the challenges of relocation.

Embrace the Challenges and Joys of Parenthood

Preparing mentally and emotionally for parenthood is crucial. The arrival of a child brings significant changes that can be both joyful and overwhelming. Journaling exercises can help you reflect on your fears and expectations. Write about what excites you and what worries you. This practice can help you process your emotions. Seeking advice from experienced parents that you admire can also be invaluable. Their insights and experiences can offer practical tips and reassurance, making you feel more prepared for the journey ahead.

Balancing responsibilities is a common challenge for new parents. Creating a schedule that balances work and family time can help manage the new responsibilities without feeling overwhelmed. Set realistic expectations for daily tasks and be flexible. Understand that it's okay if not everything gets done. Prioritize what's most important and let go of the rest. This approach can reduce stress and create a more manageable routine.

Cultivating patience and empathy towards your children and yourself is essential. Parenthood is a learning process that requires patience and understanding. Mindfulness exercises can help you stay calm during challenging moments. Take a few deep breaths before reacting to a stressful situation. Reflecting on the joys and rewards of parenting can also provide perspective. Cherishing and remembering the joyous moments can help you navigate through tough times.

Nurturing the parent-child relationship is foundational. Engaging in regular, meaningful activities together can strengthen your bond. Whether it's reading a bedtime story, playing a game, or simply talking, these moments create lasting memories and connections. I encourage you to enjoy this time with your children in a "tech-free" setting. Just as the phone can distract us from our tasks, it can also distract us from our children. Open and empathetic communication is also crucial. Actively listen to your child's thoughts and feelings with empathy and respond with understanding. This approach creates trust and mutual respect, building a strong, loving relationship.

Wisdom for Later Life

Accepting aging as a natural part of life can bring feelings of peace and fulfillment. Reflecting on the wisdom and experiences gained over the years can provide a positive perspective on aging. Consider the knowledge and insights you've accumulated and how they have shaped your life. Gratitude exercises can help you appreciate the present. Reflect on what you're grateful for each day, whether it's your health, relationships, or personal achievements. This practice can foster a sense of contentment with the inevitable passage of time.

Staying active and healthy is crucial for maintaining physical and mental well-being. Gentle exercise routines like walking or yoga can keep you physically fit and energized. These activities can also improve mental clarity and emotional well-being. Engage in mental activities like reading, puzzles, or learning new skills to keep your mind sharp and engaged. These practices can enhance your cognitive abilities and provide a sense of accomplishment.

Finding new purposes and passions in later life can bring fulfillment and joy. Volunteering or mentoring younger generations can provide a sense of purpose and connection. Sharing your knowledge and experiences can be incredibly rewarding. Pursuing hobbies or interests that were previously set aside can also bring new excitement. Whether it's painting, gardening, or traveling, these activities can enrich your life and promote a more fulfilled mindset.

Building and maintaining social connections is vital for emotional well-being. Join clubs or groups for seniors to meet new people and engage in shared activities. These connections can provide support, companionship, and a feeling of belonging. Staying in touch with family and friends through regular gatherings or calls can also strengthen your social network. These relationships offer emotional support and enrich your life, making the later years more enjoyable.

As we move forward, we will explore how to apply Stoic principles to manage difficult relationships, ensuring that you maintain your inner peace and integrity even in challenging interactions.

Chapter 5

Dealing with Difficult Relationships

"The best revenge is not to be like your enemy."

— Marcus Aurelius

Navigating difficult relationships can feel like walking a tightrope. In my last few years as a CPA, I encountered an aspiring manager who seemed to thrive on creating chaos. Recall my previous story about my old boss who lost his job to an aspiring new manager. I am referring to that same manager in this example. She spread rumors, shot down ideas that weren't hers, and maintained a consistently combative attitude in order to make everyone else feel inadequate. These interactions left me drained and questioning my professional environment. It was a turning point that pushed me to explore how Stoic principles could help me manage such toxic dynamics. So maybe I should actually consider thanking her if I ever see her again. This chapter will help you as you encounter toxic colleagues, ensuring you can maintain both your professionalism and your sanity.

Toxic Colleagues

Identifying toxic behaviors is the first step in managing difficult colleagues. Toxic colleagues often exhibit certain traits that make the work environment uncomfortable. Gossiping and spreading rumors are common behaviors. These individuals thrive on creating discord by sharing unverified information about others, damaging reputations, and nurturing a culture of mistrust. Another hallmark of a toxic colleague is undermining others' work. They may take credit for your ideas, criticize your efforts without basis, or subtly sabotage your projects. This behavior can erode your confidence and make collaboration challenging. A consistently negative attitude is another red flag. Such colleagues often complain, resist any change that isn't their idea, and focus on problems rather than solutions. Their negativity can be contagious, affecting the overall morale of the team.

Setting clear boundaries with toxic colleagues is a good way to protect your well-being. Start by communicating your limits clearly and assertively. Let your colleague know what behaviors are unacceptable and how you expect to be treated. For example, if they tend to interrupt you during meetings, calmly but firmly state, "I'd appreciate it if you could let me finish my point before responding." Being clear about your boundaries helps establish respect and reduces the likelihood of repeated negative behavior. Avoid engaging in negative conversations. Toxic colleagues often draw others into their drama. When they start gossiping or complaining, steer the conversation back to professional topics or excuse yourself. This approach protects your mental space and signals that you won't participate in such behavior, discouraging them from involving you next time.

Maintaining professionalism in all interactions with toxic colleagues is vital. Stay calm and composed during conflicts, even when provoked. Reacting emotionally can escalate the situation and undermine your credibility. Instead, take a deep breath, pause, and respond with measured words. Documenting interactions can be a valuable tool. Keep a record of incidents, including dates, times, and details of what transpired. This documentation can serve as evidence if you need to escalate the issue to HR or management. It also helps you keep track of patterns in the toxic behavior, providing a clear picture of the impact on your work environment.

Seeking support when needed is an essential aspect of managing toxic colleagues. If the situation escalates and starts affecting your productivity or mental health, it's important to involve HR or management. Reporting toxic behavior should be done with evidence. Present your documented interactions to provide a clear and factual account of the issues. This approach lends credibility to your concerns and facilitates a constructive resolution. Requesting mediation or conflict resolution can also be beneficial. Many organizations have processes in place to address workplace conflicts. Mediation involves a neutral third party who helps facilitate a resolution between you and your colleague. This process can lead to a better understanding and improved working relationship.

Reflection Section: Setting Boundaries Exercise

Think about a toxic colleague you've encountered. Reflect on the behaviors that have impacted you the most. Write down the boundaries you need to set to protect your well-being. Consider how you can communicate these boundaries clearly and assertively. Next time you interact with this colleague, practice maintaining these boundaries and observe any changes in their behavior.

By recognizing toxic behaviors, setting clear boundaries, maintaining professionalism, and seeking support when needed, you can navigate challenging relationships with greater ease. These strategies help preserve your mental and emotional well-being as well as create a healthier work environment for all.

Narcissistic Bosses

When I first encountered a narcissistic boss, I was caught off guard by his inflated sense of self-importance. He constantly sought validation and admiration from everyone around him, making it clear that he viewed himself as the linchpin of our team's success. He was also just downright mean for what seemed like no reason. A narcissistic boss often displays a lack of empathy for others, focusing solely on their own needs and achievements. This can manifest as taking credit for your work, dismissing your contributions, and showing little regard for your feelings or well-being. The need for constant admiration further complicates matters. These individuals crave praise and recognition, often manipulating situations to ensure they remain the center of attention. This behavior can create a toxic work environment, where your efforts are overshadowed by their relentless self-promotion.

Managing expectations when dealing with a narcissistic boss is crucial for maintaining your sanity. It's important to recognize that seeking personal validation from such a boss is useless. Their need for admiration often means they rarely acknowledge others' contributions. Instead, focus on what you can control—your performance and your attitude. Set realistic expectations for your interactions. Understand that their behavior is a reflection of their own insecurities and not a measure of your worth. Adjusting your expectations can help you navigate the workplace with less frustration and disappointment. As you know from my example, sometimes changing jobs can be the most beneficial thing you can do for yourself in this situation. Focus on what you can control and let the narcissists deal with their own problems.

Effective communication with a narcissistic boss requires a strategic approach. Keep your communications concise and factual. Avoid lengthy explanations or emotional appeals, as these can trigger defensiveness and manipulation. Stick to the facts and present your points clearly. Using neutral language is also vital. Phrases that are emotionally charged or confrontational can provoke a negative reaction. Instead, frame your statements calmly and objectively. For instance, rather than saying, "You never listen to my ideas," you could say, "I'd like to discuss my proposal further to ensure we're aligned." This approach reduces the risk of conflict and keeps the conversation focused on the issue at hand.

Prioritizing your own mental and emotional health is essential when dealing with a narcissistic boss. The constant need to navigate their ego can be draining. Practicing self-care outside of work becomes a vital refuge. Engage in activities that replenish your energy and bring you peace. Whether it's exercise, hobbies, or spending time with loved ones, these activities can help you decompress and maintain a balanced perspective. Additionally, seeking external support from friends, family, close colleagues, or therapists can provide valuable insights and coping strategies. Talking through your experiences with someone who understands can offer relief and validation, reinforcing that you're not alone in this struggle.

Reflection Section: Self-Care Strategies

Think about activities that bring you peace and relaxation. Write down a list of self-care strategies you can incorporate into your routine. Consider how you can carve out time each day or week to engage in these activities, prioritizing your mental and emotional well-being. Sports, movies, reading, seeing friends and family—anything that can recenter your mind on what you find important—are good choices.

By understanding the traits of a narcissistic boss, managing your expectations, communicating effectively, and prioritizing your own well-being, you can better navigate the challenges of working with such an individual. These strategies empower you to maintain your professionalism and sanity, even in a demanding and ego-driven work environment.

Conflicts at Home

Family conflicts can feel like an emotional minefield, often triggered by differing values or beliefs. Perhaps you hold a different perspective on parenting than your partner, or you and your siblings clash over political views. These differing values can create a rift, leading to frequent disagreements. Financial stress is another common source of conflict. Money issues can strain relationships, whether about budgeting, spending habits, or unexpected expenses. Finally, communication breakdowns can escalate minor disagreements into major disputes. Misunderstandings, lack of clarity, or simply not listening to each other can turn a simple conversation into a heated argument.

Practicing active listening is a powerful way to mitigate these conflicts. When you truly listen to family members, you show that you value their perspective. Active listening involves not just hearing the words but understanding the emotions and intentions behind them. Techniques for active listening include maintaining eye contact, nodding, and providing verbal affirmations like "I see" or "That makes sense." Reflecting back what's heard ensures understanding. For instance, if your partner expresses frustration about finances, you might say, "I see that you're worried about our savings. Let's talk about how we can address that." This reflection shows empathy, helps clarify the issue at hand, and lets them know their concerns are valid to you.

Using calm and neutral language during disputes can prevent escalation. "I" statements effectively express your feelings without blaming the other person. Instead of saying, "You never help with chores," you could say, "I feel overwhelmed when I have to do all the chores alone." This approach focuses on your feelings and reduces defensiveness rather than accusing the other person. Avoiding accusatory or inflammatory language is also vital. Words like "always" and "never" can make the other person feel attacked. Stick to specific behaviors rather than generalizations, and keep the conversation focused on finding a solution rather than assigning blame.

Seeking compromise and resolution is the ultimate goal in family conflicts. Start by identifying common ground and shared goals. What do you both agree on? For instance, you might both want a harmonious household, even if you have different ideas about how to achieve it. Acknowledging these shared goals can provide a foundation for compromise. Developing a plan for resolving recurring issues is the next step. If financial stress is a constant source of conflict, create a budget together and agree on spending limits. If communication breakdowns are frequent, set aside regular times to discuss important matters without distractions. This proactive approach can prevent conflicts from escalating and promote a more cooperative environment.

In my own experience, I found that addressing differing values with empathy and open-mindedness made a significant difference. For example, when my wife and I have occasionally disagreed on parenting styles, we took time to understand each other's perspectives. We used active listening to ensure we both felt heard and respected. Though there was still some disagreement, we found a middle ground that satisfied us both by focusing on our shared goal of raising happy, healthy, and mindful kids. This experience reinforced the importance of empathy, clear communication, and compromise in resolving family conflicts.

By recognizing common sources of conflict, practicing active listening, using calm and neutral language, and seeking compromise, you can navigate family disputes more effectively. These strategies help create a more harmonious home environment where conflicts are managed constructively, and relationships are strengthened.

Difficult Friends

Sometimes friendships can be challenging, especially when the dynamics become strained. You might find yourself dealing with a friend who exhibits manipulative or controlling behavior. These individuals often try to dictate your actions, making you feel obligated to comply with their wishes. This behavior can be subtle, like guilt-tripping you into doing things you're uncomfortable with, or more overt, such as making decisions on your behalf without consulting you. Another sign of a difficult friend is frequent neediness or emotional drain. These friends constantly seek your attention and support, often without reciprocating. They may call you at all hours with their problems, expecting you to drop everything to help them. Over time, this one-sided dynamic can become exhausting, leaving you feeling drained and resentful.

Communicating boundaries clearly is necessary for maintaining your well-being. When setting boundaries, it's important to use direct and compassionate language. For example, if your friend frequently calls late at night, you might say, "I value our friendship, but I need to prioritize my sleep. Can we talk during the day instead?" This approach is firm yet considerate, showing respect for both your needs and your friendship. Consistency is key when it comes to enforcing boundaries. If you've set a limit, stick to it. Inconsistency can confuse your friend and undermine the effectiveness of your boundaries. For instance, if you've decided not to answer late-night calls, don't make exceptions. Over time, this consistency reinforces your boundaries, making them more likely to be respected.

Balancing support and self-care is another essential aspect of managing difficult friendships. It's important to know when to say no. You don't always have to be available for your friend, especially if it's impacting your mental and emotional health. Politely but firmly declining unreasonable requests is a form of self-respect. You might say, "I'm sorry, I can't help with that right now. I have other commitments." Allocating time for self-care activities is vital for maintaining your well-being. Take time for yourself. You cannot effectively help others if you are not helping yourself. These moments of self-care recharge your energy, making you better equipped to support your friend when you choose to.

Evaluating the friendship's health is also necessary. Reflect on the overall impact of the friendship on your life. Does it bring you joy and support, or does it primarily cause stress and frustration? Consider the balance of give-and-take in the relationship. Healthy friendships are reciprocal, where both parties feel valued and supported. If you find the friendship is consistently draining and one-sided, it may be time to consider distancing or even ending the relationship. This decision isn't easy, but sometimes it's necessary for your well-being. Reflect on your feelings and experiences honestly. If the friendship is causing more harm than good, it might be time to move on.

Reflection Section: Friendship Evaluation

Take a moment to reflect on a difficult friendship. Write down the behaviors that have been problematic and how they've impacted you. Assess the balance of give-and-take in the relationship. Does the friendship enhance your life, or does it drain your energy? Based on this reflection, consider whether it's worth maintaining the friendship or if it's time to distance yourself.

Recognizing problematic behaviors, communicating boundaries clearly, balancing support and self-care, and evaluating friendships are essential steps in managing difficult friendships. These strategies help you navigate the complexities of interpersonal relationships with compassion and self-respect, ensuring you maintain your well-being while maintaining healthy connections.

Empathy, Understanding, and Patience

Cultivating empathy begins with practicing perspective-taking exercises. Imagine walking in someone else's shoes, experiencing their happiness, struggles, and fears. This mental exercise helps you see the world from their viewpoint, allowing for a deeper understanding of their actions and emotions. Reflect on moments when you've felt misunderstood or overlooked. Think about how a kind word or a listening ear could have made a difference. Empathy grows from recognizing shared human experiences and emotions. We all face challenges, seek happiness, and desire connection. Acknowledging this common ground helps bridge gaps in understanding, making it easier to relate to others.

Patience is a virtue, especially in interactions with difficult people. Staying calm and centered during challenging conversations can prevent escalation. Deep breathing techniques can be a lifesaver. When you feel your patience wearing thin, take a deep breath in, hold it for a few seconds, and then slowly exhale. This simple act can reset your emotional state, allowing you to respond thoughtfully instead of reacting impulsively. Recognizing and managing personal triggers is also essential. Identify the specific behaviors or situations that tend to provoke you. Understanding these triggers helps you prepare for them, making it easier to maintain your composure.

Engaging in compassionate communication is key to promoting empathy and understanding. Empathetic listening involves more than just hearing words; it's about fully engaging with the speaker's emotions and intentions. Validate their feelings by acknowledging their experiences. Phrases like "I can see why you'd feel that way" or "That sounds really tough" show that you're genuinely listening and understanding. Avoiding judgmental or critical language is equally important. Instead of saying, "You always overreact," try, "I notice that you seem really upset about this." This shift in language promotes a more open and respectful dialogue, reducing defensiveness and enabling connection.

Reflecting on personal growth can transform difficult relationships into opportunities for self-improvement. Journaling about lessons learned from interactions with challenging individuals can provide valuable insights. What did you handle well? What could you have done differently? This reflective practice helps you identify areas for growth and develop strategies for future interactions. Setting intentions for future improvements in empathy and patience can guide your actions. For example, you might decide to practice active listening more regularly or to take a moment to breathe before responding in heated situations. These small but intentional changes can significantly improve your relationships and promote personal growth.

Seeing difficult relationships as opportunities for growth can be empowering. Each challenging interaction offers a chance to practice empathy, patience, and compassionate communication. By approaching these situations with a growth mindset, you can transform adversity into a learning experience. This perspective improves your relationships and enhances your emotional resilience and self-awareness. Over time, you'll find that dealing with difficult people becomes less daunting and more manageable as you develop the skills to effectively handle these interactions.

My experience has been that taking the time to understand and empathize with others, even when it's difficult, has led to more meaningful and rewarding relationships. For instance, when working with a particularly challenging colleague, I made a conscious effort to understand her perspective and validate her feelings. Approaching these situations in such a way can de-escalate the situation and also lay the foundation for a healthy working relationship. Sometimes, people just need to be heard. By practicing these principles, you can build stronger, more empathetic connections, even in the face of challenging interactions.

By cultivating empathy, practicing patience, engaging in compassionate communication, and reflecting on personal growth, you can navigate difficult relationships with greater ease and understanding. These strategies enhance your interactions with others and also contribute to your personal development and emotional well-being. As you continue to practice these principles, you'll find that empathy and patience become second nature, enriching your relationships and creating a more compassionate and connected world.

In the next chapter, we'll explore how to find meaning and purpose in everyday life, using Stoic principles to guide our actions and decisions.

Chapter 6

Finding Meaning and Purpose

"Waste no more time arguing about what a good man should. Be one."

— Marcus Aurelius

I remember a time when I felt adrift in my accounting career. I had made some excellent progress at the firm. I just brought in and closed a huge account. It was the envy of the office, but I couldn't shake the feeling that something was missing. One evening, preparing to go home well after closing time, I found myself staring at my reflection in the window, pondering what truly mattered to me. This reflection led me to uncover my core values, which became the compass guiding my decisions and actions. Understanding what genuinely mattered to me brought a profound sense of purpose, transforming both my professional and personal life. In this chapter, we'll explore how identifying your core values can help you find deeper meaning and fulfillment.

Identify Your Core Values

We discussed core values in Chapter 3, but in this section, we will explore them a bit further and how they can help you find meaning and purpose. Core values are the fundamental beliefs that guide your decisions and behavior. They serve as the foundation of your character, shaping your interactions, choices, and priorities. When you live in alignment with your core values, you experience a sense of satisfaction and authenticity.

Common examples of core values include honesty, kindness, and integrity. Honesty involves being truthful and transparent in your dealings, creating trust and credibility. Kindness emphasizes compassion and empathy, encouraging you to treat others with respect and consideration. Integrity involves adhering to moral and ethical principles and ensuring that your actions reflect your beliefs. These values influence how you handle life's challenges, build relationships, and pursue your goals.

Reflecting on personal experiences can help you uncover your core values. Think about moments in your life that brought you significant fulfillment or caused dissatisfaction. What were the underlying reasons for these feelings? For instance, you might recall a time when you felt immense pride in helping a colleague succeed, revealing a value of collaboration and support. Conversely, a moment of frustration over a broken promise might highlight the importance you place on reliability and trustworthiness. Writing about significant life events can also provide insights into your values. Consider journaling about experiences that left a lasting impact, both positive and negative. What values were honored or violated in these moments? This reflection can help you identify patterns and themes, bringing your core values to the forefront.

Creating a values list is a practical step in this process. Compile a list of your top core values, prioritizing them to identify the most important ones. Use prompts and questions to refine your list. For example, ask yourself, "What qualities do I admire in others?" or "What principles guide my decisions during tough times?" These questions can help you delve deeper into your beliefs and identify the values that resonate most strongly with you.

Reflection Section: Create a Values List

Take a moment to reflect on your core values. Write down a list of values that are important to you. Next, prioritize these values to identify the top five that resonate most strongly with you. Use the following exercise to guide your reflection:

- What qualities do I admire in others?
- What principles guide my decisions during challenging times?
- What experiences brought me significant fulfillment or dissatisfaction?

Some examples of core values are as follows:

1. Success
2. Achievement
3. Wisdom
4. Self-Respect
5. Recognition
6. Peace
7. Leadership
8. Growth
9. Friendships
10. Faith
11. Challenge
12. Compassion
13. Authenticity
14. Meaningful work
15. Reputation

If you are still having trouble determining your core value, a quick "core values" Internet search could provide some additional insight and examples. Understanding your core values is critical, so please take some time to think these out; you will not regret it.

Aligning your values with your actions is essential for living a mean-ingful and purposeful life. Evaluate your daily habits and routines to see how well they align with your core values. For example, if one of your core values is health, yet your daily routine lacks exercise and balanced nutrition, there's a misalignment. Identifying these gaps can help you make necessary adjustments to ensure your actions reflect your values. Consider setting goals and creating a plan to integrate your values into your daily life. For instance, if kindness is a core value, you might set a goal to perform one act of kindness each day, whether it's offering a compliment, helping a neighbor, or volunteering your time. By aligning your actions with your values, you can create a more fulfilling and purpose-driven life.

Reflecting on personal experiences, creating a values list, and aligning your actions with your core values are essential steps in finding meaning and purpose. These practices help you understand what truly matters to you, guiding your decisions and actions with integrity and authenticity. As you continue to explore your values and integrate them into your life, you'll find a more profound sense of fulfillment and direction, cemented in Stoic philosophy.

Align Your Actions with Your Beliefs

Living authentically means acting in accordance with your true self—your beliefs, values, and principles. When you live authentically, you align your actions with your inner convictions, creating harmony between who you are and how you live. This alignment brings signifi-cant benefits to your mental and emotional well-being. Authenticity provides you with a sense of peace and self-respect. You feel more balanced because your actions reflect your true nature. It reduces internal conflict and boosts confidence, as you're no longer trying to meet external expectations or conform to others' standards.

Recognizing inauthentic behaviors is the first step toward living authen-tically. Inauthenticity often manifests as people-pleasing, where you prioritize others' approval over your own beliefs. This behavior can leave you feeling drained and unfulfilled, as you're constantly bending to meet others' expectations. Another common sign is self-censoring, where you suppress your genuine thoughts and feelings to avoid conflict or rejection. Reflect on moments of discomfort or internal conflict. When did you feel uneasy about a decision or action? These moments often signal a misalignment between your actions and beliefs. Understanding these signs helps you identify areas where you need to make changes.

Creating an action plan can help you align your actions with your beliefs. Start by setting specific, actionable goals for authentic living. An example being, if you value honesty but find yourself frequently agreeing to things you don't believe in, set a goal to express your true opinions more often. Break this goal into manageable steps, such as practicing speaking up in low-stakes situations or writing down your thoughts before sharing them. Create a timeline and milestones for progress. This structure provides a clear path forward and helps you stay accountable. Regularly review and adjust your goals as needed to align them with your evolving beliefs and values.

Practicing self-reflection is crucial for maintaining authenticity. Regularly take time to assess how well your actions align with your beliefs. Daily or weekly journaling prompts can be helpful for this practice. Ask yourself questions like, "Did my actions today reflect my true beliefs?" or "Where did I feel most and least genuine this week?" Reflect on your successes and areas for improvement. Celebrate the moments when you acted authentically, and identify strategies to address the times when you didn't. This ongoing reflection helps you stay true to yourself and continuously improve your alignment.

I recall a moment in my career when I struggled with inauthentic behaviors. This can be easy to do when just starting out in a new position. I often found myself agreeing with colleagues or clients, even when I disagreed with their perspectives. This led to internal conflict and dissatisfaction. Recognizing this, I set a goal to express my true opinions more confidently. I practiced in small ways, like voicing a different viewpoint during meetings or providing honest feedback to a colleague. This isn't to say I would argue with them; I would just offer a different perspective on things. Over time, these actions became more natural, and I felt a genuine sense of relief and empowerment. This experience reinforced the importance of aligning my actions with my beliefs, both for my well-being and professional integrity.

Living authentically requires courage and commitment. It involves making choices that reflect your true self, even when it's challenging. By understanding the benefits of authenticity, recognizing inauthentic behaviors, creating an action plan, and practicing self-reflection, you can align your actions with your beliefs. This alignment brings greater peace, confidence, and fulfillment, allowing you to live a life that genuinely reflects who you are. As you continue to explore and embrace authenticity, you'll find that each step brings you closer to a more fulfilling and purposeful existence.

The Power of Reflection

As we've already established, journaling is a powerful tool that can significantly enhance your self-awareness and personal growth. Putting your thoughts down on paper creates a space for introspection that can lead to profound insights. Journaling helps clarify your thoughts, making understanding your emotions and actions easier. This mental clarity can be particularly beneficial during stressful times, allowing you to process complex feelings and find solutions to your problems. Moreover, scientific studies have shown that journaling can improve emotional regulation. By regularly expressing your thoughts and feelings, you can reduce stress, anxiety, and even symptoms of depression. The act of writing itself can be therapeutic, providing a safe outlet for your emotions.

There are several techniques for journaling, each offering unique benefits. Free writing is one of the simplest methods. It involves letting your thoughts flow without any specific structure or agenda. This technique allows you to explore your subconscious mind, uncovering thoughts and feelings you might not be aware of. Set a ten to fifteen-minute timer and write whatever comes to mind. Don't worry about grammar or coherence; the goal is to let your thoughts flow freely. Structured journaling, on the other hand, involves using prompts and questions to guide your writing. This method can be beneficial if you're new to journaling or struggling with specific issues. Prompts like "What am I grateful for today?" or "What challenges did I face this week?" can provide a focused framework for your reflections.

Establishing a regular journaling routine is advised for reaping the benefits of this practice. Set aside a dedicated time each day for journaling, whether in the morning to set the tone for your day or in the evening to reflect on your experiences. I like to do this during my lunch break. Consistency is important, so choose a time that fits seamlessly into your daily schedule. Creating a comfortable and inspiring journaling space can also enhance your practice. Find a quiet spot where you won't be interrupted. Surround yourself with items that inspire you, like candles, plants, or meaningful photographs. A comfortable chair and a good-quality notebook can make the experience more enjoyable, encouraging you to stick with it.

Reflecting on your progress is an essential part of the journaling process. Periodically review your journal entries to identify patterns and recurring themes. Are there specific issues that come up repeatedly? What emotions or experiences seem to dominate your reflections? Recognizing these patterns can provide valuable insights into your thoughts and behaviors, helping you understand yourself better.

Setting new intentions based on your reflections is the next step. Use the insights you've gained to guide your future actions. If you notice that work-related stress frequently appears in your journal, consider setting intentions to manage your workload more effectively or practice stress-relief techniques. Regularly updating your goals and intentions keeps your journaling practice dynamic and aligned with your growth.

In my own life, journaling has been a transformative practice. Writing about my thoughts and feelings during stressful periods provided a much-needed release. It helps me untangle complex emotions and gain a clearer perspective on my challenges. Over time, my journal became a trusted companion, a place where I could explore my innermost thoughts without fear of judgment. This practice improved my mental clarity and enhanced my emotional resilience. By reflecting on my experiences and setting new intentions, I have been able to set specific goals for my future based on what I had learned from the past.

Cultivating a Grateful Mindset

Gratitude is a powerful catalyst for mental and emotional well-being. When you cultivate a thankful mindset, you shift your focus from what's lacking to what's abundant in your life. This simple yet profound shift can significantly improve your mental health. Studies have shown that practicing gratitude can reduce symptoms of depression and anxiety, enhance overall life satisfaction, and even improve physical health. By regularly acknowledging the positives in your life, you train your brain to seek out and appreciate more of them, creating a positive feedback loop that enhances your overall sense of well-being.

Gratitude also has a transformative effect on relationships. Expressing appreciation to others strengthens your connections and provides for more mutual respect and understanding. Acknowledging the kindness and support you receive from loved ones can deepen your bonds and create a more supportive and loving environment. This practice can also enhance your overall life satisfaction, encouraging you to focus on the positive aspects of your relationships and interactions rather than dwelling on the negatives.

As discussed in Chapter 2 regarding transforming envy into admiration, one practical way to develop gratitude is through daily gratitude journaling. As a reminder of this process, take a few moments to write down three things you're grateful for each day. These could be simple pleasures, like a warm cup of coffee in the morning, or more significant experiences, like a meaningful conversation with a friend. This exercise trains your mind to notice and appreciate the positive aspects of your day, fostering a habit of gratitude. Another effective exercise is writing gratitude letters. Think of someone who has positively impacted your life and write them a letter expressing your appreciation. This act of acknowledgment not only strengthens your relationship with the recipient but also reinforces your own sense of gratitude.

Reflecting on positive experiences before bed can also help cultivate a thankful mindset. As you wind down for the night, take a few minutes to recall the good moments of your day. This could be a kind gesture from a stranger, a task you completed, or a moment of laughter. Reflecting on these positive experiences can shift your focus away from the day's stressors and promote a sense of contentment and peace as you prepare for sleep.

Integrating gratitude into your daily life can also start with morning rituals. Begin your day with a moment of thankfulness. Before you get out of bed, think about three things you're looking forward to or are thankful for. This sets a positive tone for the day and primes your mind to seek more positive experiences. Practicing gratitude during meals or family gatherings is another effective method. Take a moment before eating to express appreciation for the food and the company. One exercise I like to do in these close group settings is ask each person to express what they feel grateful for. This can promote a sense of connectedness and enhance the enjoyment of your meals and also shift everyone's focus to positive things

Inspirational stories of individuals who have transformed their lives through gratitude can provide powerful motivation. The practice of gratitude is not limited to personal anecdotes. Historical figures have also harnessed the power of gratitude to navigate their lives. Consider the example of Helen Keller, who, despite her disabilities, often expressed her gratitude for the people who supported her and the opportunities she had. Her life is a testament to the transformative power of gratitude. By focusing on the positives, she was able to achieve remarkable feats and inspire countless others.

You can cultivate a thankful mindset by incorporating these exercises and integrating gratitude into your daily routine. This practice can transform your mental and emotional well-being, improve relationships, and enhance overall life satisfaction. The stories of individuals who have embraced gratitude are an excellent reminder of its potential to positively impact your life.

Live a Life Worth Remembering

Leaving a meaningful legacy is about the impact your actions and values have on future generations. It's not just about what you achieve professionally but also how you influence the lives of others through your character and deeds. Your legacy can take many forms—personal, professional, or philanthropic. Personal legacies often revolve around the relationships you build and the love and wisdom you share with family and friends. Professional legacies might include the innovations you bring to your field or the mentorship you provide to colleagues. Philanthropic legacies involve contributing to causes that matter to you and leaving a lasting positive impact on your community or the world.

To start envisioning the legacy you want to leave, take time to reflect on the qualities and values you want to be remembered for. What do you want people to say about you when you're no longer here? Consider writing a legacy statement or personal mission statement. This statement should encapsulate the core values and principles that guide your life. For example, you might write, "I want to be remembered as someone who always acted with integrity, compassion, and courage and made a positive difference in the lives of others." Reflecting on the qualities you admire in others can also provide insight into the legacy you wish to create. Think about the people who have left a lasting impact on you and the traits that made them memorable.

Building your desired legacy requires taking specific actions that align with your values and goals. Volunteering for causes you care about is a great way to make a difference. Whether it's mentoring young professionals, supporting local community projects, or participating in environmental initiatives, your contributions can leave a lasting impact. Mentoring or helping others in your community is another meaningful way to build your legacy. Sharing your knowledge, skills, and experiences can empower others to achieve their potential, acting as a catalyst for positive change. Identify opportunities where you can make a difference and commit to taking action regularly.

It's also important to celebrate and share your achievements along the way. Reflect on your milestones and accomplishments, acknowledging the progress you've made. This reinforces your sense of purpose and inspires others to pursue their goals. Sharing stories and lessons learned with others can be incredibly impactful. Whether through writing, speaking engagements, or casual conversations, your experiences can provide valuable insights and encouragement to those around you. By openly sharing your journey, you contribute to a legacy of wisdom and support that can benefit future generations.

Reflecting on the legacy you wish to leave and taking purposeful actions to build it can bring a profound sense of fulfillment and direction to your life. As you align your actions with your values and share your achievements, you create a lasting impact that extends beyond your lifetime. This chapter has explored various aspects of finding meaning and purpose, from identifying your core values to cultivating gratitude and building a meaningful legacy. Each of these practices contributes to a life well-lived, rich in authenticity, connection, and positive influence.

Chapter 7

Daily Practices for a Stoic Life

"When you arise in the morning, think of what a precious privilege it is to be alive - to breathe, to think, to enjoy, to love."

— Marcus Aurelius

There lies a profound opportunity to shape your day in the quiet moments before the world stirs awake. I recall a period when my mornings were chaotic, filled with the rush of getting ready for work and the anxiety of what lay ahead. During this time, I turned to the practice of morning reflections. This simple yet effective routine transformed my mornings and, consequently, my entire day. By starting with intention, gratitude, and visualization, I found a sense of calm and purpose that carried me through even the most challenging times. In this chapter, we'll explore how you can incorporate the practices we have learned so far into your morning routine to set a positive tone for your day.

This will be a great chapter to refer back to when reviewing exercises you may wish to utilize.

Morning Reflection

Starting your day with clear intentions can significantly impact your mindset and productivity. Each morning, take a few moments to reflect on your personal goals for the day. Think about what you want to achieve, both professionally and personally. Review any task lists you have made for the week to serve as a refresher on what you planned to do today. Are there specific tasks you need to complete? Are there personal interactions you want to handle with particular care? You create a roadmap for your day by identifying your goals, helping you stay focused and purposeful. Also, choose a Stoic principle to focus on. This could be something like patience, resilience, or wisdom. Let this principle guide your actions and decisions throughout the day. Writing down your intentions in a morning journal can solidify this practice. It is a tangible reminder of your goals and the Stoic principle you aim to embody.

Practicing gratitude can transform your perspective, making you more mindful of the positive aspects of your life. Begin each day by listing three things you are grateful for, or review the list you have already prepared to serve as a reminder. Reflecting on these positive aspects first thing in the morning can help you maintain a mentality of gratitude throughout the day. Gratitude has been shown to improve mental health, reduce stress, and enhance overall well-being. By making it a part of your morning routine, you start your day on a positive note, ready to face whatever comes your way with a grateful heart.

Visualizing the day ahead can help you mentally prepare for the challenges and opportunities you may encounter. Take a few moments to imagine the key events of your day. Picture yourself handling meetings, tasks, and interactions with confidence. Visualize positive outcomes, such as successfully completing a project or having a productive conversation with that difficult colleague. This mental rehearsal can boost your confidence and reduce anxiety, making you feel more prepared and in control. By envisioning a successful day, you set a positive tone and create a sense of anticipation for the opportunities ahead.

Incorporating affirmations into your morning routine can reinforce a Stoic mindset. As we discussed in Chapter 2, affirmations are positive statements that help you focus on your goals and values. Examples of Stoic affirmations include "I will focus on what I can control," "I will act with wisdom and virtue," and "I will remain calm and composed." Repeating these affirmations each morning can strengthen your resolve and keep you aligned with Stoic principles throughout the day. I mentioned that writing these on a sticky note and placing them in the bathroom or car might be a good practice. Place it somewhere you will see it every morning. Reading it in your head or speaking it out loud each morning can keep it at the forefront of your mind throughout the day. This practice can be a good reminder of your commitment to living a Stoic life.

Reflection Section: Morning Journal Prompts

To help you start your day with intention and gratitude, consider using the following prompts in your morning journal:

- What are my top three goals for today?
- Which Stoic principle will I focus on today, and how will I embody it?
- What are three things I am grateful for this morning?
- What challenges or opportunities do I anticipate today, and how will I handle them?

By reflecting on these prompts each morning, you can set a positive and purposeful tone for your day, grounded in Stoicism.

Reflect and Learn from Evening Journaling

As the day winds down, taking time to reflect on your experiences can provide valuable insights into your day's achievements or setbacks. Journaling offers a structured way to review the day's events and your emotional responses to them. At this point, you will have undoubtedly noticed how important I find journalling, as I have mentioned it several times. It really is incredibly helpful and offers a deep, raw view of yourself. Start by writing about what went well and what didn't. This practice helps you identify patterns and areas that may need improvement. Were you successful at focusing on your selected Stoic principle? Perhaps you handled that conversation with a difficult coworker gracefully, or maybe you let frustration get the best of you. By analyzing these moments, you get to know yourself a little better every day. Make sure you reward yourself for what you did right and understand that tomorrow is another opportunity to practice what you want to improve.

Identifying areas for growth is an important part of self-improvement. Reflect on moments of weakness or times when you felt you could have acted differently. What triggered those reactions? How can you improve? Setting intentions for the next day based on these reflections can help you make incremental changes. For instance, if you noticed that you were easily distracted at work, set an intention to minimize interruptions the next day. Use journaling prompts like "What did I learn today?" and "How can I improve?" to guide your reflections. These prompts encourage deeper thinking and help you focus on actionable steps for personal development.

Reinforcing the practice of gratitude at the end of the day can significantly enhance your well-being. Write about positive experiences or interactions you had, no matter how small they may seem. Recognize the small victories and progress you made. Did a colleague commend your work? Did you manage to squeeze in a workout despite a busy schedule? Acknowledging these positives can shift your focus from what went wrong to what went right, allowing for a more optimistic outlook.

Planning for the next day is another vital aspect of evening journaling. List tasks and priorities for tomorrow, ensuring they align with your short and long-term goals. Visualize a successful day ahead, imagining yourself tackling tasks with confidence and ease. By setting clear goals for the next day, you create a roadmap that guides your actions and decisions. This practice reduces morning stress and helps you start the day with a sense of direction and purpose. It also allows you to identify potential challenges and think about how to handle them, making you feel more prepared and in control.

Reflection Section: Evening Journal Prompts

Consider using the following prompts in your evening journal to guide your reflections and planning:

- What were the highlights of my day?
- What challenges did I face, and how did I respond?
- What can I learn from today's experiences?
- What are my top priorities for tomorrow?
- How can I set myself up for success in the coming day?

By incorporating these prompts into your evening routine, you encourage a habit of self-reflection and continuous improvement. Evening journaling becomes an effective tool for personal growth, helping you end each day with a sense of accomplishment and readiness for the next.

Reflecting on your day, identifying areas for growth, expressing gratitude, and planning for tomorrow can transform your evenings into a time of introspection and preparation. This practice enhances your self-awareness and fosters a mindset of continuous improvement. Evening journaling offers a structured way to process your experiences, recognize your progress, and set clear intentions for the future. I look at this as a way to make sense of a day. What made it so good, or why was it so difficult? Putting it in words on paper can provide much more insight than overthinking it.

Stoic Meditation

One of the most powerful tools in my Stoic practice has been the daily meditation on quotes from Stoic philosophers. These quotes provide inspiration and guidance, offering timeless wisdom that can be applied to modern life. Marcus Aurelius, Seneca, and Epictetus, among others, have left us with a wealth of insights that can help ground us in moments of uncertainty, stress, or confusion. Selecting a quote each day can provide a focal point for reflection and action anchoring your thoughts and intentions in the principles of Stoicism.

When you come across a Stoic quote, take a moment to reflect deeply on its meaning. Consider how it resonates with your own experiences and challenges. For instance, Marcus Aurelius wrote, "When you arise in the morning, think of what a precious privilege it is to be alive – to breathe, to think, to enjoy, to love." Reflect on this statement and think about situations where you can apply it. Perhaps you have been having difficulty expressing gratitude; how could focusing on these simple yet incredible gifts change your thinking? Writing a brief interpretation or personal connection to the quote can further deepen your understanding. Use prompts like, "How does this quote apply to my life?" or "What can I learn from this?" to guide your reflections.

Applying the wisdom of Stoic quotes to your daily life is the next step. Each quote carries a lesson that can be translated into actionable steps. If you choose Seneca's words, "Luck is what happens when preparation meets opportunity," you might set a small goal to prepare thoroughly for an upcoming project or meeting. This could involve researching, organizing your thoughts, or practicing your presentation. You turn abstract wisdom into concrete practice by setting a specific action based on the quote's message. Another example could be Epictetus' advice, "It's not what happens to you, but how you react to it that matters." You might decide to focus on maintaining composure and patience in your interactions throughout the day. These small, intentional actions can create a ripple effect, positively impacting your mindset and behavior.

Sharing and discussing Stoic quotes with others can enhance your understanding and promote meaningful connections. Discussing these insights with friends or family can provide new perspectives and deepen your appreciation of the quote's significance. For example, you might share a quote during a family dinner and invite everyone to reflect on its meaning. This can lead to enriching conversations and shared learning. Posting your reflections on social media can also create a sense of community and inspire others. Add your personal insights and encourage your network to share their interpretations. This practice reinforces your understanding and spreads Stoic wisdom, creating a broader impact.

Reflection Section: Daily Stoic Quote Practice

To integrate Stoic meditations into your daily routine, consider the following steps:

1. Choose a Stoic quote each morning from philosophers like Marcus Aurelius, Seneca, or Epictetus.
2. Reflect on the quote's meaning and how it relates to your life.
3. Write a brief interpretation or personal connection to the quote in your journal.
4. Identify a small goal or action based on the quote's message.
5. Share the quote and your reflections with friends and family or on social media to encourage discussion and deeper understanding.

Incorporating these steps into your daily practice can transform how you approach challenges and opportunities, grounding you in Stoic philosophy. By reflecting on, applying, and sharing these quotes, you can cultivate a Stoic mindset that guides your actions and decisions.

Instant Calm with Mindful Breathing

Mindful breathing can be very useful in high emotion situations, but incorporating these exercises throughout the day can also be a good practice. I like to practice breathing techniques before, during, and after work to help me keep my calm and remain focused throughout the day. The simple act of paying attention to your breath can have profound effects on your mental and physical well-being. When you practice mindful breathing, you activate your body's relaxation response, reducing stress and anxiety. This practice enhances your concentration and mindfulness, making staying present and engaged in your activities easier. By incorporating mindful breathing into your daily routine, you can create moments of calm and clarity, even amid a busy day.

One of the most basic yet practical breathing exercises is deep diaphragmatic breathing. This technique involves breathing deeply into your diaphragm rather than shallowly into your chest. To practice, sit or lie down in a comfortable position. Place one hand on your chest and the other on your abdomen. Take a slow, deep breath in through your nose, allowing your abdomen to rise as you fill your lungs with air. Your chest should remain relatively still. Hold the breath for a moment, then slowly exhale through your mouth, letting your abdomen fall. Repeat this process several times, focusing on the sensation of the breath moving in and out of your body. This technique can help calm your nervous system and bring a sense of relaxation.

Another effective breathing exercise that we have already introduced is the 4-7-8 technique. This method involves inhaling for four seconds, holding the breath for seven seconds, and exhaling for eight seconds. To begin, sit or lie down in a comfortable position. Close your eyes and take a deep breath in through your nose for a count of four. Hold the breath for a count of seven, then slowly exhale through your mouth for a count of eight. Repeat this cycle three or four times. The 4-7-8 technique can be beneficial in reducing anxiety and preparing your mind for sleep. It helps slow down your heart rate and encourages deep relaxation.

Integrating mindful breathing into your daily life can be done through specific practices. Starting your day with a morning breathing routine can set a calm and focused tone. Before you begin your daily activities, take a few moments to practice deep diaphragmatic breathing or the 4-7-8 technique. This can help center your mind and body, making you more prepared to face the day's challenges. During the day, use breathing exercises during breaks or transitions. For example, if you're moving from one task to another, take a minute to focus on your breath. This practice can help you reset and maintain a steady level of focus and energy.

Mindful breathing is also incredibly useful in moments of stress. When you find yourself in a difficult situation, pausing for a few deep breaths can make a significant difference. This brief pause lets you step back from the immediate stressor and approach the situation with a calmer, more rational mindset. For instance, if you're about to enter a high-stakes meeting or give a presentation, take a moment to practice the 4-7-8 technique. This can help calm your nerves and improve your perfor-mance. Making mindful breathing a regular practice allows you to develop a reliable tool for managing stress and maintaining your composure.

Reflection Section: Guided Breathing for Daily Calm

Consider incorporating the following guided breathing exercise into your routine to promote daily calm and focus:

1. Find a quiet, comfortable place to sit or lie down.
2. Close your eyes and take a deep breath in through your nose for a count of four.
3. Hold the breath for a count of seven, feeling the air fill your lungs.
4. Slowly exhale through your mouth for a count of eight, letting go of any tension.
5. Repeat this cycle three or four times, focusing on the sensation of the breath moving in and out of your body.

Practicing this exercise regularly can cultivate a sense of calm and clarity and refocus yourself throughout the day.

Strengthening Body and Mind with Physical Exercise

Physical exercise is not just a matter of maintaining a fit body; it is deeply intertwined with mental and emotional resilience. The Stoics believed in treating the body with respect and care, recognizing that physical health forms the foundation for a sound mind. When you engage in regular physical activity, you not only strengthen your muscles and cardiovascular system but also enhance your mental clarity and emotional stability. Exercise releases endorphins, which are natural mood lifters, and reduces levels of the stress hormone cortisol. This biochemical balance helps create a state of mental calm and focus, aligning with Stoic principles of maintaining inner tranquility amidst life's challenges.

Daily exercise routines can be simple yet highly impactful. Morning stretching or yoga exercises can set a positive tone for the day. These activities increase blood flow, improve flexibility, and prepare your body for the day's demands. A few minutes of stretching each morning can help you feel more alert and ready to take on the day. Yoga, emphasizing breath control and mindfulness, can also serve as a meditative practice, calming the mind while invigorating the body. Cardiovascular exercises like walking, running, or cycling can be incredibly beneficial for those who prefer more vigorous activity. These activities improve cardiovascular health, provide a sense of accomplishment, and boost your energy levels.

Incorporating Stoic reflection into your exercise routine can deepen its benefits. As you engage in physical activity, take the time to reflect on a Stoic quote or principle. For instance, while running or cycling, you might ponder Marcus Aurelius's words, "The impediment to action advances action. What stands in the way becomes the way." Reflecting on such wisdom can transform your workout into a time for mindful meditation, where physical exertion meets mental clarity. This practice helps you internalize Stoic teachings, making them a lived experience rather than abstract concepts. It also allows you to focus on the present moment, enhancing your awareness and connection to your body and surroundings.

Consistency in physical activity is necessary for overall well-being. Setting realistic exercise goals can help you stay committed without feeling overwhelmed. Start with achievable targets, such as walking for 30 minutes three times a week, and gradually increase the intensity and duration as you build stamina. Tracking your progress and celebrating milestones can provide motivation and a sense of accomplishment. Keep a simple exercise log where you note your activities and any improvements you notice in your strength, endurance, or mood. Celebrating these small victories reinforces the habit and encourages you to stay on track.

Reflection Section: Exercise for the Body and Mind

Consider using the following prompts to reflect on your exercise routine and its impact on your well-being:

- How does physical activity make me feel mentally and emotionally?
- Which Stoic principles could enhance my workouts?
- What are my current exercise goals, and how can I make them more achievable?
- How has regular exercise improved my overall sense of well-being?

By incorporating these reflections into your routine, you can deepen your understanding of the connection between body and mind and stay motivated to maintain regular physical activity.

As this chapter comes to a close, remember that the practices we've explored—morning reflections, evening journaling, Stoic meditations, mindful breathing, and physical exercise—are all tools to help you live a more intentional and balanced life. They offer a way to integrate Stoic principles into your daily routine, fostering resilience, clarity, and inner peace. In the next chapter, we'll delve into the art of overcoming regret and guilt, exploring how Stoic wisdom can help you move forward with grace and confidence.

Chapter 8

Overcoming Regret and Guilt

"What's done cannot be undone, but at least one can keep it from happening again."

— Seneca

I think back to one particular Saturday during tax season, I found myself sitting alone in my office, staring blankly at my computer screen. The air conditioner's hum was the only sound in the room, a stark contrast to the usual bustle of my day. As the minutes ticked by, my mind drifted to my family. It was my daughter's second birthday, and I was sitting in my office working on things far less important than the time I was missing with my daughter. Through that next week, I realized how much this regret was weighing on me, affecting my well-being and ability to focus. This chapter is dedicated to helping you understand and release your regrets, allowing you to embrace a more peaceful and purposeful life.

Understanding and Releasing Regrets

Regret can feel like an unwelcome companion, always lingering in the background. It often stems from specific events or decisions that didn't happen as planned. Reflecting on past experiences is the first step in identifying the source of your regrets. Take a moment to think about the decisions or actions you wish you could change. Perhaps it was a missed occasion, a failed relationship, or a career move that didn't go as expected. Writing down these specific regrets and their impact can provide some comprehension. Seeing your regrets in black and white helps you understand their roots and the emotions tied to them.

Holding onto regret can profoundly impact your mental and emotional well-being. The constant replay of past mistakes can lead to stress, anxiety, and even depression. According to research published in the Journal of Personality and Social Psychology, people who dwell on regrets are more likely to experience negative emotions and lower life satisfaction. Regret can hinder personal growth and happiness, as it keeps you anchored to the past, preventing you from fully engaging with the present. It can create a cycle of self-blame and doubt, making it difficult to continue forward and embrace new opportunities.

Understanding the impact of regret is a crucial step in the process of letting go. Recognize how it affects your thoughts, emotions, and behaviors. Acknowledge the toll it takes on your mental health and overall well-being. By shining a light on these effects, you can begin to see the importance of releasing regret and the potential for positive change.

Acceptance is a cornerstone of Stoic philosophy and plays a vital role in overcoming regret. The past cannot be changed, but your response to it can. Read that line one more time. Practicing acceptance allows you to acknowledge your regrets without being consumed by them. One effective Stoic exercise is reflecting on the dichotomy of control, which we touched on in Chapter 1. This concept teaches that some things are within your control, while others are not. By focusing on what you can control—your actions and responses—you can let go of the things you cannot change. Guided meditations focused on letting go can also be beneficial. These meditations encourage you to release negative emotions and cultivate inner peace.

Releasing regret through action can be an effective way to move forward. One practical step is writing a letter of forgiveness to yourself. In this letter, acknowledge the regret and its impact and offer yourself compassion and understanding. Forgive yourself for past mistakes and recognize that you did the best you could with the knowledge and resources available at the time. Performing acts of kindness can also counteract negative feelings associated with regret. Helping others can shift your focus from your own shortcomings to the positive impact you can have on the world. Engaging in a symbolic act of release, such as writing your regrets on paper and burning them, can provide a tangible sense of closure. This act can be a powerful reminder that you are choosing to let go of the past and embrace the present.

Reflection Section: Releasing Regret

Take a moment to reflect on a specific regret that has been weighing on you. Write down the event or decision that caused the regret and its impact on your life. Next, write a letter of forgiveness to yourself, acknowledging the regret and offering compassion. Consider performing a symbolic act of release, such as writing the regret on paper and burning it to provide a sense of closure. This exercise can help you understand, accept, and release your regrets, allowing you to move forward with a lighter heart and clearer mind.

Practice Self-Forgiveness

In the quiet moments when the day's responsibilities have faded, the echo of past mistakes can sometimes grow louder. Acknowledging these "cringe moments," as I like to call them, is the first step toward self-forgiveness. It's important to own your mistakes without self-judgment. Start by journaling about the mistake and its impact. Write down what happened, how it made you feel, and its consequences on your life. Reflect on the context and reasons behind the mistake. Consider the circumstances you were in, the information you had at the time, and the pressures you faced. Understanding these factors can provide a clearer picture and reduce the harshness of self-criticism.

Compassion is a powerful antidote to self-blame. Treat yourself with the same kindness you would offer a friend in a similar situation. Imagine a close friend coming to you with the same mistake. How would you respond? Likely with empathy and understanding. Apply this same compassion to yourself. Engage in self-compassionate journaling exercises, where you write supportive and understanding letters to yourself. Use positive self-talk and affirmations to counteract negative thoughts. Guided self-compassion meditations can also help. These meditations focus on cultivating a sense of kindness toward yourself, helping break the self-blame cycle.

Making amends, when possible, can be a significant step in the healing process. Begin by apologizing to those affected by your mistake. A sincere apology acknowledges the hurt caused and shows a willingness to take responsibility. Express your regret and desire to make things right. If appropriate, offering to compensate for the mistake can also demonstrate your commitment to rectifying the situation. This might involve repairing a damaged relationship, making financial restitution, or simply acknowledging the hurt and promising to do better in the future. Making amends is not just about easing the other person's pain; it's also about finding closure and moving forward with a clear conscience.

Moving forward requires a plan to avoid repeating the same mistakes. Set specific goals for personal improvement. These goals should be realistic and actionable, allowing you to make measurable progress. For example, if your mistake involved poor communication, set a goal to practice active listening and clear expression in your interactions. Seek support or mentorship to guide you. A mentor can provide valuable insights and help you navigate challenges. Reflecting on the lessons learned from your mistake is equally important. Write down the insights gained and how they have shaped your character. Apply these lessons to future actions, ensuring continuous and meaningful growth.

Reflection Section: Creating an Action Plan

1. Identify a mistake you want to address.
2. Write down the specific actions you can take to make amends.
3. Set three specific, realistic goals for personal improvement related to the mistake.
4. Identify a mentor or support system to help guide you if necessary.
5. Reflect on the lessons learned and how they can be applied in the future.

Learn from Mistakes and Turn Guilt into Growth

Continuing our reflections on mistakes, think about a time when you made a significant error. It may have been a decision at work that didn't pan out or a personal misstep that hurt someone you care about. Write about what you learned from that experience. How did it shape your character? It may have taught you the value of patience or underscored the importance of listening before acting. You can gain clarity and perspective by putting your reflections into words, turning a painful memory into a valuable lesson. This process helps you understand that mistakes are not failures but growth opportunities.

Guilt, while often seen as a negative emotion, can actually serve as a motivator for positive change. Instead of letting guilt weigh you down, use it as a catalyst for setting goals for personal growth and improvement. Channel this guilt into constructive actions. For instance, if you feel guilty about neglecting a friendship, make a conscious effort to reach out and rebuild that connection. If guilt stems from a professional mistake, seek out additional training or mentorship to enhance your skills. Transforming guilt into motivation propels you forward, turning a source of pain into a driving force for betterment.

Sharing your story can be immensely liberating. Writing about your journey in a blog or journal allows you to process your emotions and offer insights that might help others. Consider speaking about your experiences in support groups or forums. Your story can serve as a beacon of hope for those grappling with similar issues. It creates a sense of community and shared understanding, reinforcing that everyone makes mistakes and that growth is a universal journey. When you share your experiences, you become an example, inspiring others to learn from their own missteps and move forward with renewed vigor.

Adopting a growth mindset is vital for turning mistakes into opportunities for development. View each mistake as a stepping stone rather than a stumbling block. Practice gratitude for the lessons learned. Even the most painful experiences can offer valuable insights. Set intentions for continuous self-improvement. This might involve committing to regular self-reflection or seeking out new learning opportunities. Reflect on your personal growth and progress over time. Keep a journal where you document your achievements and the lessons learned along the way. This practice tracks your development and reinforces the idea that growth is a continual process.

Embrace the Here and Now

Mindfulness is an exceptional tool to help you stay engaged in the present moment. One way to practice mindfulness is through the mindful breathing exercises we learned in the previous chapter. These simple exercises can calm your mind and bring you back to the present.

There are other mindfulness techniques that can also be incredibly effective. Guided mindfulness meditations lead you through a series of steps to help you focus on your body, breath, and surroundings, creating a sense of inner peace. Another method is mindful walking or eating. When walking, focus on each step, the sensation of your feet touching the ground, and the rhythm of your movement. Similarly, when eating, savor each bite, notice the flavors, and chew slowly. One exercise I like to do when taking a trip or visiting somewhere new is to close my eyes and take a deep breath of the fresh air right when I get out of the car. This helps me to relax and reminds me that I am in a new place to enjoy. These practices can transform simple activities into moments of mindfulness.

Shifting your focus from the past to the present can significantly improve your well-being. Reflect on the benefits of living in the present. When you focus on the here and now, you reduce stress and anxiety about things that have already happened or might happen in the future. Setting daily intentions to stay present can help reinforce this mindset. Each morning, decide to focus on the present throughout your day. Remind yourself to bring your attention back to the current moment whenever you notice your mind wandering. This practice can help you develop a habit of present-centered thinking, leading to a more present and focused life.

Immersing yourself fully in daily activities can also help you stay present. Practice single-tasking instead of multitasking. When you focus on one task at a time, you can give it your full attention and do it more effectively. Avoid the temptation to juggle multiple tasks simultaneously, as this can lead to decreased productivity and increased stress. Find joy in simple, everyday moments. Whether it's enjoying a cup of tea, listening to your favorite music, or spending time with loved ones, fully engage in these activities. Allow yourself to experience the pleasure and satisfaction of being present in the moment.

Minimizing distractions is crucial for maintaining focus on the present. Start by creating a distraction-free environment. Arrange your home or workspace to be clean and organized, free from unnecessary clutter. This can help reduce visual distractions and create a sense of calm. Setting boundaries for digital device use is also important. Designate specific times for checking emails, scrolling on social media, and other digital activities. Turn off notifications when you are focused on being present in the moment. By limiting the constant influx of digital distractions, you can maintain your attention on the present and savor every moment of it.

Embracing mindfulness, adopting a present-centered mindset, engaging fully in daily activities, and minimizing distractions can transform your daily life. These practices help you stay grounded, reduce stress, and find joy in the present moment. As you incorporate these strategies into your routine, you'll likely notice a positive mental and emotional well-being shift. You'll become more aware of your surroundings, more engaged in your activities, and more content with your life.

Positive Affirmations to Rewrite Your Inner Script

Understanding the power of affirmations begins with recognizing their ability to reshape negative thought patterns. Our brains are incredibly adaptable, a quality known as neuroplasticity. This means that the thoughts you consistently focus on can actually rewire your brain over time. When repeated regularly, positive affirmations can help form new neural pathways that reinforce a more optimistic and resilient mindset. Research in cognitive psychology supports this, showing that affirmations can reduce stress, increase well-being, and improve performance.

In college, I had a friend who struggled heavily with self-doubt. She began using affirmations like "I am capable and confident" every morning. Without even knowing it, she was practicing Stoic philosophy. Over time, she saw a change in her attitude and school performance, which ultimately helped her graduate. She continues to use these practices today and has told me several times that she attributes part of her career success to these affirmations.

Crafting personalized affirmations that resonate with you is vital to their effectiveness. Start by identifying the negative thoughts that frequently occupy your mind. Perhaps you often think, "I'm not good enough," or "I always mess things up." Transform these negative statements into positive, present-tense affirmations. For example, replace "I'm not good enough" with "I am worthy and capable of achieving my goals." Make sure your affirmations are phrased positively and in the present tense. Instead of saying, "I will be successful," say, "I am successful." This subtle change encourages your brain to perceive these statements as current truths, making it easier to internalize them.

Incorporating affirmations into your daily routine can amplify their impact. Repeating them during your morning or evening routines helps set a positive tone for the day or gives a sense of closure and peace before sleep.

Visualization is a powerful tool that can enhance the effect of your affirmations. Guided visualization exercises can help you imagine the positive outcomes of your affirmations. For instance, if you're using the affirmation "I am confident in public speaking," spend a few minutes each day visualizing yourself speaking confidently in front of an audience. Picture the details—how you stand, the sound of your voice, the reactions of the audience. Creating a vision board that reflects your affirmations can also be highly effective. Gather images and words that represent your goals and place them on a board where you can see them daily. This visual representation keeps your affirmations and goals at the forefront of your mind, motivating you to take actions that align with them.

You can effectively rewrite your inner script by understanding the power of affirmations, personalizing them to resonate with your unique challenges and aspirations, integrating them into your daily life, and enhancing them with visualization techniques. This process helps cultivate a more positive and resilient mindset, releasing thoughts of guilt or regret and replacing them with a focus on personal growth and fulfillment. As we move forward in the book, we will explore the concept of balancing modern life, drawing on Stoic principles to find harmony and purpose amidst the chaos of our fast-paced world.

Chapter 9

Balancing Modern Life

"Life, if well lived, is long enough."

— Seneca

When my daughter was a baby, I read an article describing how young children constantly glance at their parents to seek approval. The article's main point was about phone use and how we cannot connect with our children if our noses are constantly buried in our phones. I realized the parent described in the article was similar to me, perpetually attached to my device yet increasingly disconnected from what was happening right in front of me. My cell phone was the first thing I reached for in the morning and the last thing I saw before sleep. The endless stream of texts, notifications, and constant scrolling on social media turned a source of unwinding into a source of stress. I was always on, always available, and always exhausted. It was this point that led me to explore the concept of a digital detox. This chapter is dedicated to helping you understand the impact of excessive screen time on your mental and emotional health and providing practical steps to reduce it.

Reduce Screen Time for Mental Clarity

The impact of excessive screen time on mental and emotional health cannot be overstated. Studies have shown that prolonged exposure to screens is linked to increased levels of stress, anxiety, and sleep disturbances. The blue light emitted by screens interferes with our circadian rhythms, making it harder to fall asleep and stay asleep. Social media, too, plays a significant role in this equation. Research indicates that excessive use of social media can lead to feelings of inadequacy, loneliness, and depression. The constant comparison with others' curated lives can erode our self-esteem and contribute to a pervasive sense of dissatisfaction.

To mitigate these effects, it is crucial to set clear digital boundaries. One effective strategy is to create tech-free zones or times, which I introduced in Chapter 3. Consider making your bedroom a screen-free sanctuary to improve your sleep quality. Implement digital-free evenings where you and your family disconnect from devices and engage in meaningful face-to-face interactions. Additionally, using apps to monitor and limit screen time like "Moment" or "Screen Time" allows you to track your usage and set specific time limits for social media use. You can regain control over your digital consumption by being mindful of your screen time and setting boundaries.

Engaging in offline activities can also provide a fulfilling alternative to screen time. Hobbies like reading, gardening, or painting offer a sense of achievement and relaxation. Spending time outdoors, whether walking in the park or hiking in the mountains, can rejuvenate your mind and body. Physical activities release endorphins, which boost your mood and reduce stress levels. Practicing mindfulness or meditation can help you stay present and grounded, providing a much-needed respite from the digital noise. These activities enrich your life and create a healthy balance between the online and offline worlds.

Reflection Section: Offline Activities Checklist

- Make a list of hobbies or activities you enjoy but have neglected due to screen time.
- Schedule at least one offline activity each day for the next week.
- Reflect on how these activities make you feel and any changes in your stress levels or mood.

A gradual approach to digital detox is often more sustainable and manageable. Start by making small, manageable changes to your routine. For example, reduce your screen time by 15 minutes each day. Gradually increase these offline periods as you become more comfortable with the change. Reflect on the benefits you notice over time, such as improved sleep, reduced stress, and feeling more present in your daily life. Keeping a journal can help you track your progress and stay motivated. Document your experiences, noting any positive changes in your mental and emotional well-being.

By understanding the impact of screen time, setting digital boundaries, engaging in offline activities, and implementing a gradual detox plan, you can reclaim your mental clarity and emotional health. Remember, the goal is not to eliminate technology from your life but to create a balanced relationship with it. This balance can lead to a more fulfilling, peaceful, and purposeful life, free from the constant demands of the digital world.

Integrate Stoicism into Your Career for Work-Life Balance

Balancing work and personal life is a challenge many face. Often, the demands of our careers can overshadow our personal needs, leading to burnout and dissatisfaction. One practical approach to finding balance involves clarifying your personal and professional priorities. Reflect on your core values and consider how they align with your career goals. For example, if integrity and family are important to you, ensure your job allows you to act ethically and spend quality time with loved ones. Creating a list of top priorities for work and personal life can be a daily reminder of what truly matters. This list helps you stay focused and make decisions that align with your values.

Establishing and maintaining healthy workplace boundaries is necessary for preserving your mental and emotional well-being. It starts with communicating your availability and limits to colleagues and supervisors. Let them know when you are available for meetings and when you need uninterrupted time to focus. Scheduling regular breaks throughout the day is also crucial. These breaks allow you to reset and recharge, preventing burnout. Respecting your personal time means only checking work emails or taking calls during off-hours if absolutely necessary. Prioritizing tasks and delegating can also help manage your workload more effectively. By setting boundaries, you create a more balanced and sustainable work environment.

Integrating mindfulness practices into your workday can significantly reduce stress and improve focus. Taking mindful breaks, even if just for a few minutes, can help you reset and recharge. During these breaks, practice deep breathing exercises to calm your mind and reduce stress. Reflecting on your daily achievements and areas for improvement can also provide value. At the end of the day, carve out some time to acknowledge what you accomplished and identify any areas where you can improve. By incorporating mindfulness into your routine, you can navigate the demands of your job with greater ease and clarity.

Achieving a healthy work-life balance requires creating a balanced daily schedule that includes time for work, family, and self-care. Start by setting realistic goals for what you can achieve each day. Avoid overcommitting yourself, as this can lead to unnecessary stress. Reflect on the balance you have achieved at the end of each week and make adjustments as needed. For instance, if you find work is encroaching on your personal time, reassess your schedule and set firmer boundaries. Engaging in activities that bring you joy and relaxation, such as spending time with family, exercising, or pursuing hobbies is essential for maintaining overall well-being. One of my favorite quotes a coworker shared with me is, "You can't pour from an empty cup." It's such a simple yet profound statement. If you don't take care of yourself, you can't take care of other things. You can create a more fulfilling and productive life by prioritizing self-care and personal time.

Reflection Section: Priorities and Boundaries Checklist

1. Reflect on your core values and career goals. List your top five personal and professional priorities.
2. Communicate your availability and limits to colleagues and supervisors.
3. Schedule regular breaks and respect your personal time.
4. Prioritize tasks and delegate when possible.
5. At the end of each week, reflect on the balance achieved and adjust your schedule as needed.

Balancing work and personal life is an ongoing process that requires continuous reflection and adjustment. By clarifying your priorities, setting boundaries, practicing mindfulness, and maintaining a balanced schedule, you can integrate Stoic principles into your career and create a more harmonious and fulfilling life. Remember, the goal is not to achieve perfection but to find a sustainable and meaningful balance that aligns with your values and promotes overall well-being.

Apply Minimalism to Simplify Your Life for Greater Peace

Minimalism is more than just a trend; it is a philosophy that deeply aligns with Stoic principles of simplicity and focus. At its core, minimalism emphasizes the importance of eliminating excess to make room for what truly matters. This approach offers numerous benefits for mental clarity and emotional well-being. By stripping away the non-essential, you can focus on the things that bring value and joy to your life. This clarity can reduce stress and realign your perspective, helping you navigate daily challenges with a clear mind and a centered heart.

One of the first steps in embracing minimalism is decluttering your physical space. Your surroundings have a significant impact on your mental state. A cluttered environment can lead to a cluttered mind, making concentrating difficult and increasing stress levels. Begin by simplifying different areas of your home. Start with your wardrobe. Go through each item and ask yourself if it still serves a practical purpose or creates joy. The KonMari method, popularized by Marie Kondo, suggests keeping only those items that spark joy. This approach can be very liberating, allowing you to let go of possessions that no longer serve you. Move on to other areas like the kitchen, workspace, and garage. Creating a calm and organized living space sets the stage for a more peaceful and focused life.

Simplifying your schedule is another crucial aspect of minimalism. In our fast-paced world, it is easy to become overwhelmed by a never-ending to-do list. Begin by identifying and eliminating non-essential activities. Reflect on your core values and prioritize tasks that align with them. This may involve saying no to commitments that do not serve your long-term goals or values. You can focus on what truly matters by creating a balanced and manageable daily schedule. I think back to a social media post my wife shared with me. It said something like, "As teenagers, we would look forward to being invited to parties on the weekends; as adults, we dread it." She viewed this post's meaning from an introvert's perspective. I viewed it from the perspective of someone who is already too busy to add something else to their calendar. Declining an invitation may be difficult, but it is also sometimes necessary.

Adopting a minimalist mindset extends beyond your physical space and schedule. It involves shifting your focus from possessions to experiences. In a consumer-driven society, equating happiness with material wealth is easy. However, true fulfillment often comes from meaningful experiences and connections. Practice gratitude for what you have rather than constantly seeking more. Reflect on the impact of minimalism on your overall well-being. You may find that by owning less, you gain more—more time, more peace, and more joy. This shift in perspective can lead to a more fulfilling and intentional life grounded in the values that matter most to you.

Manage Money with a Stoic Mindset

In my early career, I often grappled with financial stress before adopting Stoic principles. The pressure to keep up with colleagues, the lure of immediate gratification, and the relentless pursuit of more left me constantly feeling on edge and inadequate. After discovering Stoicism, I studied the principles to find a more balanced and rational approach to managing my finances.

Adopting a Stoic approach to finances can immediately transform your relationship with money. At its core, Stoicism emphasizes moderation and the avoidance of excess. This principle is particularly relevant in a consumer-driven society where the temptation to overspend is ever-present. Practicing moderation means making thoughtful and intentional financial decisions, focusing on needs over wants. It involves asking yourself whether a purchase truly adds value to your life or simply serves as a fleeting source of pleasure. By developing this mindset, you can create a financial discipline prioritizing long-term stability over short-term gratification.

Creating a budget is a practical step toward achieving financial stability. Begin by tracking your income and expenses to understand your financial situation clearly. This process involves documenting all sources of income and categorizing your expenses into essentials, discretionary spending, and savings. Setting financial goals and priorities is crucial. Determine what you want to achieve, whether building an emergency fund, paying off debt, or saving for a major purchase. Allocate funds accordingly, ensuring your essentials are covered and a portion is set aside for savings. This structured approach allows you to take control of your finances and make informed decisions that align with your goals.

Practicing financial discipline is vital for maintaining stability. One of the key habits to nurture is avoiding impulsive purchases. In moments of temptation, pause and reflect on whether the purchase aligns with your financial goals and values. Building an emergency fund is another critical aspect of financial discipline. Aim to save at least three to six months' worth of expenses to cushion yourself against unexpected financial setbacks. Reducing debt and avoiding unnecessary credit can also contribute to your financial well-being. Prioritize paying off high-interest debts and avoid accumulating new debt unless absolutely necessary. When practiced consistently, these habits create a solid foundation for financial stability.

Investing wisely is another important element of managing your finances with a Stoic mindset. Begin by researching investment options and understanding the associated risks. Diversifying your investments is an excellent way to minimize risk and maximize potential returns. This means spreading your investments across different asset classes, such as stocks, bonds, and real estate, to reduce the impact of any single investment's poor performance. Seeking advice from financial experts can provide valuable guidance and is recommended if you're new to investing. Consult with a financial advisor to develop a personalized investment strategy that aligns with your goals and risk tolerance. You can build a portfolio that supports your long-term financial objectives by making thoughtful and informed investment decisions.

Reflection Section: Budgeting Template

1. **Income:** List all sources of income (salary, bonuses, side jobs).
2. **Expenses:** Categorize into essentials, discretionary spending, and savings.
3. **Financial Goals:** Define short-term and long-term goals (emergency fund, debt repayment, major purchases).
4. **Allocation:** Allocate funds to each category, ensuring essentials are covered and savings are prioritized.
5. **Tracking:** Regularly review and adjust the budget to stay on track.

By integrating Stoic principles into your financial decisions, you can cultivate a sense of moderation and intentionality that promotes long-term stability. Creating a budget, practicing financial discipline, and investing wisely are all steps that can help you achieve financial well-being. Remember, the goal is not to accumulate wealth for its own sake but to create a balanced and secure financial foundation that supports your overall well-being and aligns with your values.

Build Supportive Relationships

Recognizing the importance of community is essential for a balanced and fulfilling life. Strong relationships have a profound impact on our mental and emotional well-being. Studies show that individuals with robust social networks experience lower stress and anxiety levels and higher levels of happiness and life satisfaction. The Stoic principle of interconnectedness and mutual support emphasizes that we are all part of a larger whole. By fostering connections with others, we not only enrich our own lives but also contribute to the well-being of our community. This sense of belonging and shared purpose aligns with the Stoic belief that we are social beings designed to support and uplift one another.

Community activities are a great way to build and strengthen these connections. Volunteering for local organizations or causes can provide a sense of purpose and fulfillment. Whether it's helping out at a food bank, participating in community clean-up efforts, or mentoring youth, these activities allow you to make a tangible difference in the lives of others. Joining clubs, groups, or classes with shared interests is another excellent way to connect with like-minded individuals. Whether it's a board game group, a recreational sports team, or an art class, these gatherings provide opportunities to form meaningful bonds. Attending community events and gatherings, such as local festivals, farmers' markets, or neighborhood meetings, can also help you stay connected and engaged with those around you.

Building meaningful connections requires more than just participation; it involves nurturing deep and supportive relationships. Practicing active listening and empathy is crucial in this regard. When genuinely listening to others and striving to understand their perspectives, you create a space for trust and mutual respect. Being present and engaged in interactions means putting aside distractions and giving your full attention to the person you are with. This presence creates a deeper connection and shows that you value the relationship. Offering support and encouragement to others, whether through words or actions, strengthens these bonds. By being there for others in need, you create a support network that uplifts and sustains you when you find yourself in need.

Reflecting on the impact of your community involvement can provide valuable insights and reinforce the importance of these connections. Take time to write about your experiences and the relationships you have formed. Consider how these connections have enriched your life and contributed to your growth. Setting intentions for continued community engagement can help you stay committed to nurturing these relationships. Reflect on how giving back to your community benefits others and brings a sense of purpose and fulfillment to your own life. This reflection can inspire you to seek out new opportunities for involvement and deepen your existing connections.

Reflection Section: Community Impact

1. Take a moment to write about a recent community activity you participated in.
2. Reflect on the connections you made and the impact it had on you and others.
3. Set intentions for future community engagement, considering new ways to contribute and connect.

Recognizing the importance of community and actively participating in it can lead to a more balanced and full life. By engaging in meaningful activities, building deep and supportive relationships, and reflecting on the impact of your involvement, you can cultivate a sense of belonging and purpose that aligns with Stoic principles. This interconnectedness enriches not only your life but also the lives of those around you, creating a compounding effect of positivity and support. As you continue to explore the principles of Stoicism, remember that your connections with others are a vital part of your journey toward peace and purpose.

Chapter 10

Inspirational Stoic Stories and Quotes

"The impediment to action advances action. What stands in the way becomes the way."

— Marcus Aurelius

W hen I first encountered the teachings of Marcus Aurelius and Seneca, it was like finding a roadmap to peace of mind. I had been grappling with a series of personal doubts that left me feeling adrift and empty. I was up late one evening dreading going to bed and waking up the next morning for another Monday at the office. I was flipping through "Meditations" by Marcus Aurelius. The weight of his words resonated with me, offering a different perspective than the one I was used to. It made me realize that even though his words were written almost two thousand years ago, their meaning is still relevant to many of the events and challenges we face daily. This chapter delves into the lives and writings of these ancient Stoics, exploring how their teachings can illuminate our modern lives.

Lessons from Ancient Stoics

Marcus Aurelius, often referred to as the philosopher-king, ruled as a Roman Emperor from 161 to 180 AD. His reign was marked by military conflict, political turmoil, and personal loss. Yet, despite the immense pressures of his position, Marcus found solace and strength in Stoic philosophy. His private journal, "Meditations," offers a profound glimpse into his inner life and Stoic mindset. Written during his military campaigns, these reflections were never intended for publication. They allowed Marcus to practice self-examination and maintain his moral compass amidst the challenges of the time.

Key themes in "Meditations" include resilience, humility, and duty. Marcus often reminded himself of the transient nature of life, encouraging a focus on what truly matters. He wrote, "You have power over your mind—not outside events. Realize this, and you will find strength." This passage underscores the Stoic principle of focusing on what is within our control. Marcus cultivated resilience and inner peace by accepting the impermanence of external circumstances. His reflections on humility are equally compelling. Despite his status, Marcus acknowledged his human frailties and the limits of his power. He often reflected on the interconnectedness of all people, emphasizing that true leadership is rooted in service to others.

Marcus Aurelius' role as an emperor put his Stoic beliefs to the test. During the Antonine Plague, which ravaged the Roman Empire, his leadership was crucial. Marcus remained composed and focused on his responsibilities despite the fear and uncertainty. His writings during this period reflect his unwavering commitment to duty and the Stoic virtue of courage. He urged himself and others to face adversity with calm and rationality. This steadfastness in the face of calamity is a testament to the practical application of Stoic principles.

Seneca, another prominent Stoic philosopher, served as an advisor to Emperor Nero. His life was marked by political intrigue, personal exile, and eventual forced suicide. Seneca's writings exude a profound sense of wisdom and tranquility despite his life's hardships. His letters and essays offer practical advice on living a virtuous and fulfilling life. In "Letters from a Stoic," Seneca addresses a wide range of topics, from managing time to dealing with adversity. He emphasized the importance of rational thought, writing, "We suffer more often in imagination than in reality." This insight encourages us to recognize the power of our minds in shaping our experiences.

Seneca's practical lessons extend to managing time and cultivating inner peace. In "On the Shortness of Life," he laments the tendency to squander time on trivial pursuits. He urges us to seize each moment, stating, "It is not that we have a short time to live, but that we waste a lot of it." This emphasis on the efficient use of time is particularly relevant in today's fast-paced world. We can lead more meaningful and focused lives by prioritizing what truly matters and eliminating distractions.

Seneca's life was filled with challenges. He was exiled to Corsica for eight years, a period that tested his Stoic resolve. Instead of succumbing to despair, Seneca used this time to reflect and write. His exile became a catalyst for personal growth and philosophical exploration. Eventually, he returned to Rome, where he continued to navigate the treacherous political landscape. Seneca's ability to maintain his composure and integrity in the face of adversity is a powerful example of Stoic resilience.

The teachings of Marcus Aurelius and Seneca offer timeless wisdom that is deeply relevant today. Marcus Aurelius' reflections on mindfulness can help us manage modern stressors. By accepting there are things we cannot control, we can shift our focus to things that truly matter. Seneca's advice on time management is equally pertinent. His call to prioritize and use time wisely can guide us toward a more balanced and fulfilling life in a world filled with constant distractions.

Reflection Section: Applying Stoic Wisdom Today

Consider a current challenge or stressor in your life. Reflect on how Marcus Aurelius' focus on what is within our control or Seneca's advice on managing time can offer a new perspective. Write down your reflections and any actionable steps you can take to apply these Stoic principles.

The lives and writings of Marcus Aurelius and Seneca illuminate the power of Stoic philosophy to navigate life's complexities. Their teachings on resilience, humility, duty, and time management provide practical guidance for modern challenges. By embracing their wisdom, we can develop a more balanced, purposeful, and resilient mindset, finding strength and serenity amidst the uncertainties of everyday life.

Modern Practitioners of Stoicism

The principles of Stoicism are not confined to ancient texts and philosophers. Today, there are modern practitioners who embody these teachings in their daily lives, offering a contemporary lens through which we can understand and apply Stoic wisdom. Individuals like Ryan Holiday and Tim Ferriss have brought Stoicism into the mainstream, demonstrating its relevance in the modern world. Ryan Holiday, a best-selling author and marketing strategist, has written extensively about Stoic philosophy. His books, such as "The Daily Stoic" and "The Obstacle Is the Way," offer practical advice on incorporating Stoic principles into everyday life. Tim Ferriss, an entrepreneur and author of "The 4-Hour Workweek," has also embraced Stoicism, often discussing its impact on his personal and professional life on his podcast and blog.

These well-known figures are not alone. Everyday individuals from various walks of life have shared their own Stoic journeys, showing how these ancient principles can guide us through contemporary challenges. Take, for example, a business leader who uses Stoic principles to navigate corporate challenges. Decisions must be made quickly and often under immense pressure in the high-stakes business world. This leader starts each day with a morning routine inspired by Stoic reflections. He begins with a few moments of meditation, focusing on a specific Stoic quote. This practice helps him maintain clarity and composure throughout the day. During stressful meetings or negotiations, he recalls the Stoic teaching to focus on what he can control and let go of what he cannot. By applying these principles, he has cultivated a reputation for being calm, rational, and fair, even in the most challenging situations.

Athletes, too, have found Stoicism to be a valuable framework for maintaining focus and resilience. Consider an endurance athlete who competes in ultra-marathons. These races are a test of physical strength and mental fortitude. The athlete employs Stoic techniques to stay grounded and focused during grueling training sessions and races. Before each race, she engages in negative visualization, a Stoic practice where one imagines the worst-case scenarios to prepare mentally for any outcome. This exercise reduces her fear of the unknown and helps her stay calm when unexpected challenges arise. During the race, she uses Stoic principles to manage pain and fatigue, reminding herself that while she cannot control the conditions of the race, she can control her response to them. This mindset has enabled her to push through physical and mental barriers, achieving feats she once thought impossible.

Stoicism also provides practical tools for individuals overcoming personal adversity. One example is a woman who faced significant life changes after a divorce. Initially overwhelmed by the emotional turmoil, she turned to Stoic teachings for guidance. She began incorporating Stoic journaling into her daily routine, reflecting on her thoughts and emotions through the lens of Stoic principles. This practice helped her gain perspective and identify areas where she could take constructive action. By focusing on what was within her control, such as her attitude and reactions, she gradually rebuilt her life with a sense of purpose and resilience. Stoic techniques for managing stress, like deep breathing and mindfulness, became essential tools in her daily life. Over time, she found that Stoicism helped her navigate the immediate crisis and equipped her with skills to handle future challenges with greater confidence and composure.

The practical applications of Stoicism these individuals use highlight its versatility and effectiveness. Morning routines inspired by Stoic reflections can set a positive tone for the day, promoting mental clarity and focus. Techniques for managing stress, such as negative visualization and mindfulness, help build emotional resilience. Incorporating Stoic journaling into daily life encourages self-reflection and personal growth. These practices are accessible and can be tailored to fit various lifestyles and needs. Integrating Stoic principles into your routines allows you to develop a more balanced and intentional approach to life.

The impact of practicing Stoicism is profound. Those who embrace these teachings often report increased mental clarity and focus. Focusing on what is within their control makes them less likely to be overwhelmed by external stressors. This clarity allows them to make more rational and informed decisions, enhancing their personal and professional lives. Emotional resilience is another significant benefit. Stoic practices help individuals build a solid inner foundation, enabling them to navigate life's ups and downs more easily. They become better equipped to handle adversity and recover from setbacks, maintaining inner peace and stability.

Improved relationships are another positive outcome of practicing Stoicism. Individuals can foster more profound and meaningful connections by cultivating virtues like patience, empathy, and humility. They learn to communicate more effectively, listen actively, and respond thoughtfully. This approach strengthens existing relationships and attracts new, positive connections. Personal fulfillment is the most rewarding aspect of embracing Stoicism. Individuals find a greater sense of purpose and contentment by aligning their actions with their core values and focusing on what truly matters. They can live more authentically, guided by principles that resonate deeply with their inner selves.

The stories and practices of modern Stoic practitioners illustrate the timeless relevance of Stoic philosophy. Whether navigating corporate challenges, enduring physical feats, or overcoming personal adversity, Stoicism offers practical tools and insights that can transform our lives. Incorporating these principles into your daily routine can cultivate mental clarity, emotional resilience, improved relationships, and personal fulfillment. Stoicism is not just an ancient philosophy; it is a living, breathing practice that can guide us through the complexities of modern life.

Wisdom for Daily Life

Amid life's turbulence, Stoic quotes can provide a beacon of wisdom and clarity. These concise yet profound statements encapsulate the essence of Stoic philosophy, offering guidance and inspiration. Marcus Aurelius, Seneca, Epictetus, and other Stoic philosophers have left us a treasure trove of quotes that resonate with timeless wisdom. By curating a collection of these quotes, you can create a source of daily inspiration and reflection.

Consider the words of Marcus Aurelius: "The happiness of your life depends upon the quality of your thoughts." This quote underscores the Stoic emphasis on the power of the mind in shaping our experiences. This reminder to focus on our internal landscape is invaluable in today's world, where external circumstances often feel overwhelming. Reflect on this quote in the context of modern challenges. When faced with stress or adversity, consider the quality of your thoughts. Are they constructive, or are they feeding your anxiety? You can cultivate a more positive and resilient mindset by consciously directing your thoughts.

Seneca's wisdom also offers profound insights. He once said, "If a man knows not to which port he sails, no wind is favorable." This quote highlights the importance of setting goals for your life based on our core values. Without guidance, it is easy to feel overwhelmed and lost. Every path we take can feel like the wrong one. By setting goals that align with your core values, uncertainty becomes decisiveness. Reflect on this quote when you feel lost or unsure about significant life decisions. Instead of taking an easy path you are uncertain of, consider other paths that may align better with your goals and core values. This perspective can provide direction through some of life's most difficult decisions.

Epictetus, another revered Stoic philosopher, reminds us that challenging situations can often feel more complicated than they actually are. He said, "Man is not worried by real problems so much as by his imagined anxieties about real problems." This quote encapsulates the Stoic practice of mindfulness. In times of distress, whether it's a challenging work situation or a personal crisis, remember not to let your mind make the problem appear worse than it really is. Reflect on this quote when you face anxiety-inducing difficulties. Practice the techniques we previously discussed - mindful breathing, rational analysis, and Stoic visualization. This approach can transform what appears to be a mountain into a molehill.

Reflection

Analyzing these quotes can deepen your understanding and help you apply their wisdom to your life. Take Marcus Aurelius' quote on the quality of thoughts. Its deeper significance lies in the recognition that our internal state profoundly influences our external reality. This insight is particularly relevant in the age of social media, where constant comparison can erode self-esteem. You can navigate the digital landscape with greater resilience by cultivating positive and constructive thoughts.

Seneca's quote on setting goals emphasizes the importance of aligning goals with core values. Reflecting on this, you might realize that many of your achievements that have brought joy to your life did so because they aligned with your core values. This understanding can shift your focus from what is most accessible to what works best for you. In your career, for instance, this could mean turning down that promotion to spend more quality time with your family. You create a much more fulfilled life by aligning your goals with your core values.

Epictetus' quote on anxiety speaks to the heart of Stoic emotional management. Its relevance is evident in everyday situations, such as a fear of failure or embarrassment in school or the workplace. Reflect on how you view seemingly overwhelming situations. Do you let those situations become mountains in your way, or do you cut them down to size with Stoic mindfulness? Your mind is an incredible tool. If you guide it correctly, you can approach every situation with calm and clarity.

Application

To integrate these Stoic quotes into your daily life, consider setting intentions based on their wisdom. For example, after reflecting on

Marcus Aurelius' quote about thoughts, you might set an intention to practice mindfulness. This could involve daily meditation to observe and guide your thoughts. Over time, this practice can help you develop a more positive and focused mindset.

Using quotes as daily affirmations can also anchor your day in Stoic principles. Start your morning by reading a quote and repeating it to yourself. Let's take Seneca's quote on goal setting. Begin your day with the affirmation: "If a man knows not to which port he sails, no wind is favorable." This mantra can motivate you to set goals for your day and focus on achieving them.

Meditation prompts inspired by Stoic quotes can further deepen your practice. For instance, meditate on Epictetus' quote about anxiety. Spend a few minutes each day reflecting on how you can improve your responses to the situations that may pop up during the day, big and small. Remember to focus on visualizing the positive outcomes of these situations instead of all the things that can go wrong. This exercise can help you internalize the Stoic approach to adversity, making it a natural part of your behavior.

Daily Practice

Incorporating Stoic quotes into your routine can be a powerful tool for personal growth. Create a daily practice of reading and reflecting on a Stoic quote. You might start a journal dedicated to these reflections. Each day, write down a quote and explore its meaning. Consider how it applies to your current life situation and what actions you can take based on its wisdom. Revisit your daily entries occasionally and reflect on your achievements. Did the quote successfully help you in a particular situation? Can you apply this quote to a new issue you are facing?

Reflection Section: Daily Quote Practice

Begin today by selecting a Stoic quote that resonates with you. Write it down in a journal and spend a few minutes reflecting on its meaning. Consider how it applies to your current situation and what steps you can take to embody its wisdom. Share your reflections with friends or on social media to inspire others and foster shared growth.

Incorporating Stoic quotes into your daily life can provide a steady source of inspiration and guidance. By reflecting on their deeper significance, setting intentions, and sharing their wisdom, you can build a more mindful and resilient approach to life. These small but consistent practices can transform your mindset. I encourage you to try this, and I promise you will not be disappointed.

Share Your Journey

Your Story Matters

As we reach the final pages of _"Modern Stoicism"_, I hope the wisdom we've explored together has brought you closer to the calm, resilience, and inner peace you seek in life.

If the teachings and practices shared throughout this book have touched your life, helped you navigate challenges, or provided you with moments of clarity and strength, I would be honored to hear about your experience. Your feedback is not only valuable to me, but it also has the power to guide and inspire others on their journey toward emotional strength and fulfillment.

I invite you to take a moment to leave a review on Amazon.com. Whether it's a Stoic principle that resonated deeply with you or the overall impact the book has had on your perspective, your review can encourage others to embark on their own path toward a more Stoic and peaceful life. It only takes a few minutes and can make a lasting difference.

Just leave a review on Amazon.com by visiting the link below:

https://www.amazon.com/review/review-your-purchases/?asin=B0DHD8FZL8

You can also scan this QR code with the camera on your phone and touch the link that pops up. The rest is even easier. Just follow the prompts to leave your review.

Thank you for spending time with my work and for embracing the journey of personal growth and transformation. Your words can become a source of guidance for others seeking balance and emotional strength in their own lives.

With deep appreciation,

J. T. Wells

Remember, your reflections could be the key that helps someone else unlock the power of Stoicism. If you're comfortable, share a snippet of how Stoic philosophy has influenced your thinking or your favorite lesson from the book.

Conclusion

As we come to the end of this book, let's take a moment to reflect on the core themes and lessons we've explored together. We began by delving into the rich history of Stoicism, understanding its roots in the Hellenistic period and its evolution through the Roman Empire. We examined the lives of prominent Stoic philosophers like Zeno of Citium, Marcus Aurelius, and Seneca, who laid the foundation for this enduring philosophy.

Throughout the chapters, we explored how the Cardinal Virtues of Stoicism—wisdom, courage, justice, and temperance—can be applied to various aspects of modern life. From managing emotions and building self-discipline to navigating life transitions and dealing with difficult relationships, Stoic teachings offer practical tools for overcoming life's challenges. We also looked at finding meaning and purpose, balancing modern life, and drawing inspiration from Stoic stories and quotes.

The key takeaways from this book are simple yet profound. First, focus on what you can control and accept what you cannot. This principle, known as the dichotomy of control, is central to Stoic philosophy and can help you maintain inner peace regardless of external circumstances.

Second, practice self-reflection and mindfulness to better understand your emotions and reactions. By doing so, you can respond to situations with clarity and composure. Third, cultivate resilience by embracing challenges as opportunities for growth. Lastly, align your actions with your core values to live a life of integrity and authenticity.

On a personal note, I'd like to share a final thought with you. In both the accounting world and my banking career, I've faced my fair share of high-pressure situations and professional setbacks. Stoicism has been my anchor, helping me maintain a clear and focused mindset. I can say with certainty that I still struggle, I still have setbacks, and I still stumble on my path toward a Stoic life. But that is ok. All of us will fail at this. The goal is not to never fail; the goal is to get up and keep going when we do. The idea of a Stoic Sage is just that, an idea. We will never attain that title, nor should we strive to do that. But I can promise that if you take these lessons to heart and practice the exercises I gave you, you will improve your situation. It is a time-tested fact that these principles work.

Now, I encourage you to take specific steps to integrate Stoic principles into your life. Start by setting aside time each day for self-reflection and journaling. Reflect on your actions, emotions, and thoughts, and consider how they align with your core values. Practice mindfulness and gratitude to stay grounded in the present moment. Embrace challenges as opportunities for growth, and focus on what you can control. Doing so will cultivate inner peace, resilience, and a sense of purpose.

I recommend further reading and resources for those who wish to deepen their understanding of Stoicism. "Meditations" by Marcus Aurelius offers timeless wisdom and personal reflections on Stoic principles. "Letters from a Stoic" by Seneca provides practical guidance on ethics and overcoming adversity. "The Daily Stoic" by Ryan Holiday and Stephen Hanselman is an excellent resource for daily reflections and meditations.

I want to leave you with an inspirational quote from Epictetus that has stuck with me for a long time: "How long are you going to wait before you demand the best for yourself?" It's a simple question with what should be a simple answer. I believe the time is here and now. By taking this journey with me, I believe you also feel that is the answer. You have already made the first step by trying to gain more understanding of Stoicism from this book. Now, it is up to you to take the next.

Thank you for embarking on this journey with me. I hope you find solace, strength, and purpose in the teachings of Stoicism. Remember, you have the power to change your life by changing your perspective. Embrace the wisdom of the Stoics, and let it guide you toward a more peaceful and purposeful existence.

Resources

Aurelius, M. (2003). *Meditations: A New Translation* (G. Hays, Trans.). Random House Publishing Group.

Bailey, C. (2019, November 26). *5 Research-based strategies for overcoming procrastination*. Harvard Business Review. https://hbr.org/2017/10/5-research-based-strategies-for-overcoming-procrastination

Brooks, J. (2022, September 6). *My insanely productive stoic morning journal routine*. The Stoic Handbook. https://www.stoichandbook.co/my-insanely-productive-stoic-morning-routine

Brooks, J. (2023a, February 16). *The ultimate stoic daily routine*. The Stoic Handbook. https://www.stoichandbook.co/ultimate-stoic-daily-routine

Brooks, J. (2023b, June 26). *How to let go of anger: Seneca's 16 Stoic techniques*. HighExistence. https://www.highexistence.com/seneca-on-how-to-deal-with-anger

Burton, N. (2024, June 26). *How to cope with fear and anxiety, the Stoic way*. Psychology Today. https://www.psychologytoday.com/us/blog/hide-and-seek/202203/how-to-cope-with-fear-and-anxiety-the-stoic-way

Calm Editorial Team. (2024, February 9). *8 Tips to help you cultivate an attitude of gratitude.* Calm Blog. https://www.calm.com/blog/attitude-of-gratitude

Daily Stoic. (2017, November 25). *Marcus Aurelius quotes.* https://dailystoic.com/marcus-aurelius-quotes

Daly, B. (2023, November 7). *Why has Stoicism gained popularity in modern times?* The Collector. https://www.thecollector.com/why-has-stoicism-gained-popularity-in-modern-times

Durand, M., Shogry, S., & Baltzly, D. (2023, January 20). *Stoicism.* Stanford Encyclopedia of Philosophy. https://plato.stanford.edu/entries/stoicism

Eichinger, B. (2024, May 13). The connection between excessive screen time and mental health issues. *Nexus Health Systems.* https://nexushealthsystems.com/excessive-screen-time-mental-health-issues

Epictetus. (2022). *The complete works: Handbook, Discourses, and Fragments.* University of Chicago Press.

Forbes, A. (2024, June 23). The beliefs of Stoicism: Ethics, principles and practical applications. *Of Mind And Body.* https://ofmindandbody.com/the-beliefs-of-stoicism-ethics-principles-and-practical-applications

Forbes Coaches Council. (2021, February 1). *16 Ways to achieve work-life balance by setting better boundaries.* Forbes. https://www.forbes.com/councils/forbescoachescouncil/2021/02/01/16-ways-to-achieve-work-life-balance-by-setting-better-boundaries

Ho, L. (2023, December 6). *11 SMART Goals Examples for Life Improvement.* LifeHack. https://www.lifehack.org/864427/examples-of-personal-smart-goals

Holiday, R. (2019, August 7). *How to recover from a breakup: Timeless lessons from the Stoics.* Daily Stoic. https://dailystoic.com/how-to-recover-from-a-breakup-timeless-lessons-from-the-stoics

Holiday, R. (2020, November 28). *Meditations by Marcus Aurelius: book summary, key lessons and best quotes*. Daily Stoic. https://dailystoic.-com/meditations-marcus-aurelius

Holiday, R. (2022, March 7). *Tim Ferriss on cultivating resilience, favorite stoic practices and how to shun comfort*. Daily Stoic. https://dailystoic.com/tim-ferriss

Isaac. (2023, June 24). *Stoics on jealousy: Powerful advice for overcoming jealousy*. The Realized Man. https://rb.gy/p4qftm

Jain, A. (2024, March 7). How to Overcome Regret with Stoicism - Atul Jain - Medium. *Medium*. https://medium.com/@laserjet1000/how-to-overcome-regret-with-stoicism-7cacbf1d249e

Ken. (2020, August 31). *Letters from a Stoic by Seneca: book summary, key lessons and best quotes*. Daily Stoic. https://dailystoic.com/letters-from-a-stoic

LeBon, T. (2023, April 23). *The Stoic dichotomy of control in practice*. Psychology Today. https://www.psychologytoday.com/us/blog/365-ways-to-be-more-stoic/202304/the-stoic-dichotomy-of-control-in-practice

Monk, H. (2017, March 9). 5 Stoic principles for modern living. *Pocket-Stoic*. https://medium.com/pocketstoic/5-stoic-principles-for-modern-living-applying-an-ancient-philosophy-to-the-21st-century-2a8e10f31887

Polat, B. (2017, November 4). *Happy families: A Stoic guide to family relation-ships*. Modern Stoicism. https://modernstoicism.com/happy-families-a-stoic-guide-to-family-relationships-by-brittany-polat

Robertson, D. J. (2022, December 10). *An ancient stoic meditation technique*. https://donaldrobertson.name/2017/03/22/an-ancient-stoic-medita-tion-technique

Sadler, G. (2018, June 9). *Dealing with Difficult People at Work: Stoic Strategies*. Modern Stoicism. https://modernstoicism.com/dealing-with-difficult-people-at-work-stoic-strategies-by-greg-sadler

Salzgeber, J. (2020, January 15). *Train your mind to adapt to any circumstance.* NJlifehacks. https://www.njlifehacks.com/train-mind-to-adapt-to-any-circumstance

Scroggs, L. (n.d.). *Time blocking.* Todoist. https://todoist.com/productivity-methods/time-blocking

Seneca, L. (2020). *Letters from a Stoic (Collins Classics).* William Collins.

Stoic Simple. (n.d.-a). *Stoic philosophy & aging: How Stoicism helps in getting older.* https://www.stoicsimple.com/stoic-philosophy-aging-how-stoicism-helps-in-getting-older

Stoic Simple. (n.d.-b). *Stoicism & personal finance: Stoic philosophy for financial stability.* https://www.stoicsimple.com/stoicism-personal-finance-stoic-philosophy-for-financial-stability

Stoicism (Stanford Encyclopedia of Philosophy). (2023, January 20). https://plato.stanford.edu/entries/stoicism/#:~:text=1.1%20The%20School%20and%20its%20History,-The%20Stoic%20school&text=Zeno%20was%20succeeded%20in%20the,its%20foremost%20theorist%20and%20systematizer.

Stoicism, W. I. (2022, January 4). 9 Morning affirmations to set up a stoic day - Stoicism — Philosophy as a way of life - medium. *Medium.* https://medium.com/stoicism-philosophy-as-a-way-of-life/9-morning-affirmations-to-set-up-a-stoic-day-77f65df7d400

Stoicminds Channel. (2023, July 27). Stoic wisdom for dealing with difficult people and toxic relationships. *Medium.* https://medium.com/@stoicminds.channel/stoic-wisdom-for-dealing-with-difficult-people-and-toxic-relationships-f068a660051f

Sutton, J., PhD. (2024, July 15). *15 Values worksheets to enrich clients' lives (+ inventory).* PositivePsychology.com. https://positivepsychology.com/values-worksheets

Team: Solo Admin. (2023, October 18). *From stress to success: Using Stoic principles to thrive in the workplace.* https://www.teamsoloadmin.com/using-stoic-in-the-workplace

Travers, M. (2023, June 30). 5 Mental health rewards of embracing minimalism, according to a psychologist. *Forbes*. https://www.forbes.com/sites/traversmark/2023/06/28/5-mental-health-rewards-of-embracing-minimalism-according-to-a-psychologist

Voncken, B. (2024, August 4). *How to forgive like a Stoic*. Via Stoica. https://viastoica.com/how-to-forgive-like-a-stoic

What is Stoicism. (2022, January 4). *9 Morning affirmations to set up a stoic day*. Medium. https://medium.com/stoicism-philosophy-as-a-way-of-life/9-morning-affirmations-to-set-up-a-stoic-day-77f65df7d400

Made in the USA
Las Vegas, NV
21 December 2024

15007564R00072